VEGETABLE JOTTER Dr. D.

Other Books in the JOTTER Series:
ROSE JOTTER · HOUSE PLANT JOTTER

Year:	Location:

                                                                              page

CHAPTER 1   **INTRODUCTION** 2–6
                      Crop Rotation.. 2
                      Basic Rules.. 3
                      Basic Facts.. 4–5
                      Vegetable Plot Plan... 6

CHAPTER 2   **VEGETABLES A–Z**............................... 7–54

CHAPTER 3   **CARE**... 55–61
                      Buying Seed . Intercropping
                      Growing Under Cloches . Manuring....................... 55
                      Thinning . Transplanting
                      Mulching . Earthing-up . Feeding 56
                      Watering . Weeding . Storing............................... 57
                      Pests & Diseases... 58–59
                      Cultural Control . Chemical Control 60
                      General Disorders 61

CHAPTER 4   **DIARY & ACKNOWLEDGEMENTS**........... 62–64

pbi PUBLICATIONS · BRITANNICA HOUSE · WALTHAM CROSS · HERTS · ENGLAND

All rights reserved. No part of this publication may be reproduced, stored in a retrieval system, or transmitted in any form or by any means whatsoever without the prior written permission of the copyright holder.

Printed and bound by Hazell Watson and Viney Limited Aylesbury Bucks. England

ISBN 0 903505 28 2   © D G HESSAYON 1989

CHAPTER 1
INTRODUCTION

How to use this book
On each page you will find scores of facts to help you with your plants. Check up each time you decide to buy or have a new job to do. On many of the pages there are sections which are printed in blue — these are for you to fill in with your own information. In this way you can build up a permanent record and a useful reminder for next year.

Raising your own vegetables has a fascination for millions of men and women throughout the country. You *can* save money by growing vegetables — it has been estimated that an expenditure of £1 yields crops worth about £9 at shop prices. But saving money is not the main motive for most people — there are more important reasons for growing food in the garden.

First of all there is the enjoyment of an active and healthy hobby — plus the satisfaction of eating the product of your own labour. In addition there are more practical benefits. The crop can be harvested at the peak of tenderness and flavour instead of having to wait for maximum yields like the professional grower. You can grow vegetables which never appear in the shops and you can grow top-flavour varieties of ordinary vegetables which farmers never grow. You can also serve vegetables within an hour or two of picking and with sweet corn, asparagus, chicory, beans etc that means a new flavour experience.

It takes a well-run plot of about 100 sq.yd to keep one person supplied with all his or her vegetable requirements (except potatoes) for a whole year. At the other end of the scale a few tubs or growing bags on a patio can provide fresh tomatoes, french beans, courgettes and new potatoes. Either way, there is the thrill of growing your own.

CROP ROTATION

You should not grow a vegetable in the same spot year after year. If you do then soil troubles are likely to build up, and the level of nutrients will become unbalanced. Crop rotation is the answer, and the standard 3 year plan is shown here. A strip of land at one end of the plot is sometimes used for permanent crops (rhubarb, asparagus etc) and is left out of the plan. Not everyone is willing to follow this rotation plan, and regrettably all idea of a rotation is abandoned. It would be much better to follow a very simple rotation — roots this year, above-ground crops next year and then back to root crops.

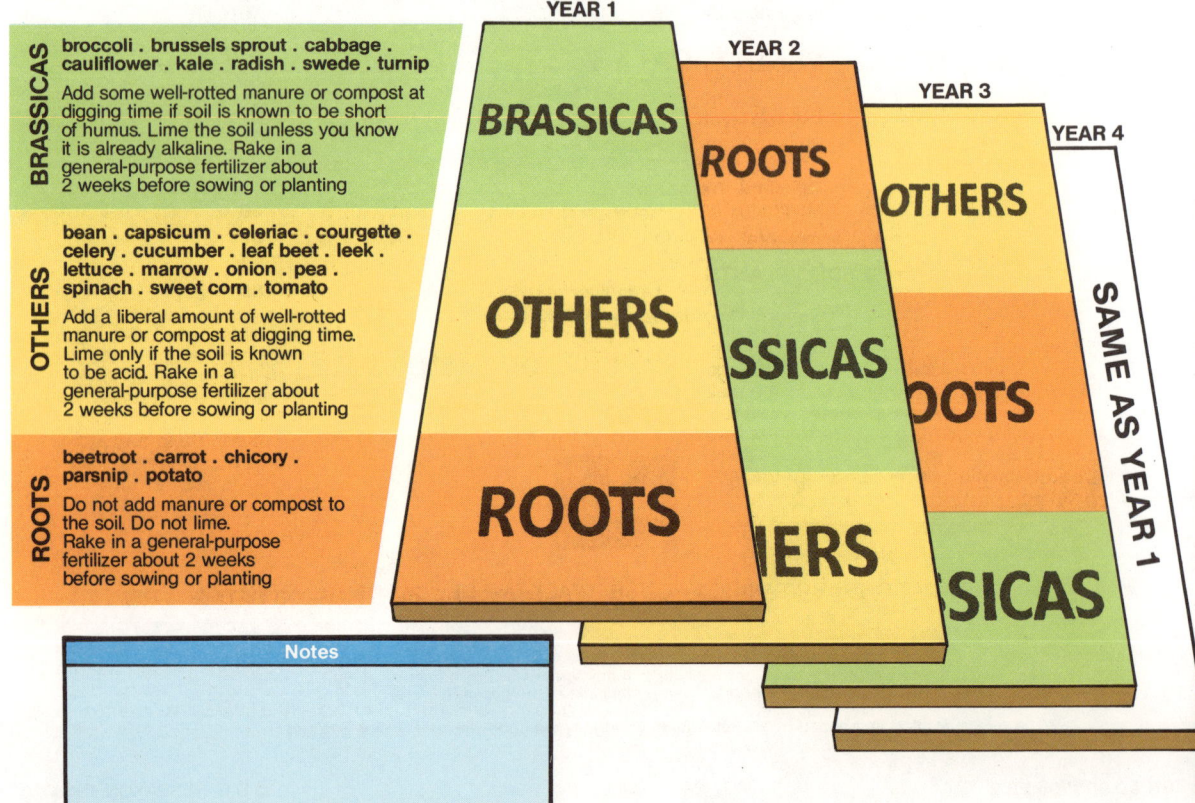

BRASSICAS
broccoli . brussels sprout . cabbage . cauliflower . kale . radish . swede . turnip

Add some well-rotted manure or compost at digging time if soil is known to be short of humus. Lime the soil unless you know it is already alkaline. Rake in a general-purpose fertilizer about 2 weeks before sowing or planting

OTHERS
bean . capsicum . celeriac . courgette . celery . cucumber . leaf beet . leek . lettuce . marrow . onion . pea . spinach . sweet corn . tomato

Add a liberal amount of well-rotted manure or compost at digging time. Lime only if the soil is known to be acid. Rake in a general-purpose fertilizer about 2 weeks before sowing or planting

ROOTS
beetroot . carrot . chicory . parsnip . potato

Do not add manure or compost to the soil. Do not lime. Rake in a general-purpose fertilizer about 2 weeks before sowing or planting

Notes

BASIC RULES

1. DIG EARLY
Don't try to dig and make a seed bed in one operation. The time for digging is during a dry spell in late autumn or early winter if you intend to sow or plant in the spring. Choose a spade which is suited to your height and strength — keep the blade clean. Begin slowly — about 30 minutes is quite enough for the first day. Insert the blade vertically, not at an angle. Leave the soil in lumps — frost will break down the clods during winter.

Digging Notes

2. PREPARE A PROPER SEED BED
In early spring the soil will become workable — moist but not sticky. Now is the time to make a seed bed. The first job is to break down the clods — use a hand cultivator or a garden fork, working on a push-pull principle across the surface. Now rake in a dressing of fertilizer and then walk over the surface with a rake, using the implement and not your feet to fill in the hollows and break down the mounds. Pick up debris and small stones. The final step is to use the rake in a push-pull fashion to produce a smooth and level seed bed with a crumbly surface.

3. BUY GOOD QUALITY SEEDS & PLANTS
Always obtain good quality seed, and don't leave ordering to the last minute. Store the packets inside a tin with a tight lid in a cool place. Sometimes you will need to buy seedlings instead of seeds for transplanting into the plot. Choose carefully — the plants should be sturdy, green and with a good root system. Here you *should* leave it to the last minute, because there must be a minimum delay between purchase and planting.

Buying Notes

4. SOW NON-STORABLE CROPS LITTLE & OFTEN
Several vegetables such as lettuce, radish and cabbage cannot be stored for later use. To avoid gluts and famines it is wise to sow a short row every few weeks. A boon for the busy (or lazy) gardener are the 'mixed seed' packets of lettuce, radish etc offered by many seed suppliers. The mixture of early- and late-maturing varieties gives a protracted harvesting period from a single sowing.

5. SOW & PLANT AT THE PROPER TIME
Proper timing is extremely important. The calendars in this book will give you the approximate times for sowing and planting — soil and weather conditions determine the exact time. The soil must be moist but it must not be wet and waterlogged. Remember the basic seed sowing rule — not too early, not too deeply, not too thickly. The traditional method is to sow the seed in drills, marking the ends with sticks. In recent years the bed system has become increasingly popular — the seeds are sown in a block rather than in drills so that all plants are the same distance from each other. Spacings are quite close so that the leaves of mature plants touch each other.

6. THIN PROMPTLY & ENSURE RAPID GROWTH
Remove weeds and thin the seedlings as soon after germination as practical. Overcrowding at this early stage can be crippling. Firm the plants after thinning and gently water to settle the disturbed roots. The growing plants must be watered and fed if necessary to ensure rapid growth. Water shortage and starvation are common causes of leathery leaves, premature running to seed, woody roots and lack of flavour.

7. TACKLE PROBLEMS PROMPTLY
Inspect the plants regularly and at the first sign of trouble look up the cause on page 58. For a more detailed description of vegetable troubles consult The Vegetable Expert. Once you have put a name to the problem, act quickly. Many pests and diseases can be checked quite easily if treated promptly, but may be difficult or impossible to control if left to get out of hand. It is a good idea to keep a small selection of pesticides in the garden shed for emergency use. Keep them away from children and read the instructions before spraying.

8. PICK MOST CROPS EARLY & OFTEN
You may be surprised at some of the harvesting times recommended in this book — turnips the size of a golf ball and carrots no longer than a finger. But the young stage is often the peak time for tenderness and flavour. With some crops such as marrows, cucumber, peas and beans it is essential to pick regularly as just a few mature fruits or pods left on the plant can bring cropping to an end.

BASIC FACTS

Vegetable	Easy or difficult	Number of seeds per ounce	Expected germination time	Life expectancy of seed	Time from sowing to harvest	Time from planting to harvest	Page number
ARTICHOKE, GLOBE	Not easy — needs space & attention	—	—	—	—	1½ years	8
ASPARAGUS	Not easy — needs space & attention	—	—	—	—	2 years	9
BEAN, BROAD	Easy	15	7–14 days	2 years	Spring sowing: 14 weeks Autumn sowing: 26 weeks	—	10–11
BEAN, FRENCH	Easy	60	7–14 days	2 years	8–12 weeks	—	12–13
BEAN, RUNNER	Easy, but support & constant picking necessary	30	7–14 days	2 years	12–14 weeks	8–10 weeks	14–15
BEET, LEAF	Easy	2000	10–14 days	3 years	12 weeks	—	16
BEETROOT	Easy	2000	10–14 days	3 years	Globe vars: 11 weeks Long vars: 16 weeks	—	17
BROCCOLI	Moderately easy	8000	7–12 days	4 years	Green vars: 16 weeks Other vars: 44 weeks	Green vars: 10 weeks Other vars: 38 weeks	18
BRUSSELS SPROUT	Moderately easy if soil is suitable	8000	7–12 days	4 years	Early vars: 28 weeks Late vars: 36 weeks	Early vars: 22 weeks Late vars: 30 weeks	19
CABBAGE	Moderately easy	8000	7–12 days	4 years	Spring vars: 35 weeks Summer vars: 20 weeks	Spring vars: 29 weeks Summer vars: 14 weeks	20–21
CAPSICUM	Difficult	4000	14–21 days	5 years	18 weeks	10 weeks	22
CARROT	Moderately difficult	20,000	17 days	4 years	Early vars: 12 weeks Maincrop vars: 16 weeks	—	23
CAULIFLOWER	Difficult	8000	7–12 days	4 years	Summer vars: 18 weeks Winter vars: 46 weeks	Summer vars: 12 weeks Winter vars: 40 weeks	24–25
CELERIAC	Moderately difficult	70,000	12–18 days	5 years	35 weeks	28 weeks	26
CELERY	Difficult	70,000	12–18 days	5 years	Trench vars: 40 weeks Self-blanching vars: 25 weeks	Trench vars: 32 weeks Self-blanching vars: 17 weeks	27
CHICORY	Moderately easy	20,000	7–14 days	5 years	18–30 weeks	—	28
COURGETTE	Moderately easy	150	5–8 days	6 years	10 weeks	8 weeks	29

Vegetable	Easy or difficult	Number of seeds per ounce	Expected germination time	Life expectancy of seed	Time from sowing to harvest	Time from planting to harvest	Page number
CUCUMBER, GREENHOUSE	Difficult	75	3–5 days	6 years	14 weeks	10 weeks	30
CUCUMBER, OUTDOOR	Difficult	75	6–9 days	6 years	14 weeks	12 weeks	31
KALE	Easy	8000	7–12 days	4 years	35 weeks	29 weeks	32
LEEK	Easy, but occupies land for a long time	10,000	14–18 days	3 years	Early vars: 30 weeks Late vars: 45 weeks	Early vars: 22 weeks Late vars: 37 weeks	33
LETTUCE	Moderately easy if rules are followed	20,000	6–12 days	3 years	8–14 weeks	—	34–35
MARROW, SQUASH & PUMPKIN	Moderately easy	150	5–8 days	6 years	14 weeks	12 weeks	36
ONION & SHALLOT from sets	Easy	Onion: 5 Shallot: 2	Sprout in 11–14 days	—	—	18–20 weeks	37
ONION from seed	Moderately easy if proper seed bed is prepared	8000	21 days	1–2 years	Spring-sown vars: 22 weeks Summer-sown vars: 46 weeks	—	38–39
PARSNIP	Easy	8000	10–28 days	1 year	34 weeks	—	40
PEA	Difficult	75	7–10 days	2 years	12–16 weeks	—	41–43
POTATO	Moderately easy	½–1 seed potato	Sprout in 6 weeks	—	—	Early vars: 13 weeks Maincrop vars: 22 weeks	44–45
RADISH	Easy	3000	4–7 days	6 years	Summer vars: 3–6 weeks Winter vars: 10–12 weeks	—	46
SPINACH	Moderately easy if rules are followed	1500	12–20 days	4 years	8–14 weeks	—	47
SWEDE	Easy	8000	6–10 days	3 years	20–24 weeks	—	48
SWEET CORN	Moderately easy in right location	100	10–12 days	2 years	14 weeks	—	49
TOMATO, GREENHOUSE	Moderately difficult	7000	8–11 days	3 years	20 weeks	12 weeks	50–51
TOMATO, OUTDOOR	Difficult	7000	8–11 days	3 years	20 weeks	12 weeks	52–53
TURNIP	Easy	8000	6–10 days	3 years	6–12 weeks	—	54

VEGETABLE PLOT PLAN

Draw the outline of your plot and mark the position of the rows on the plan. Write in the names of the vegetables along the lines. Alternatively you can note each reference (e.g D–6 to N–6) on the appropriate page of the A–Z guide.

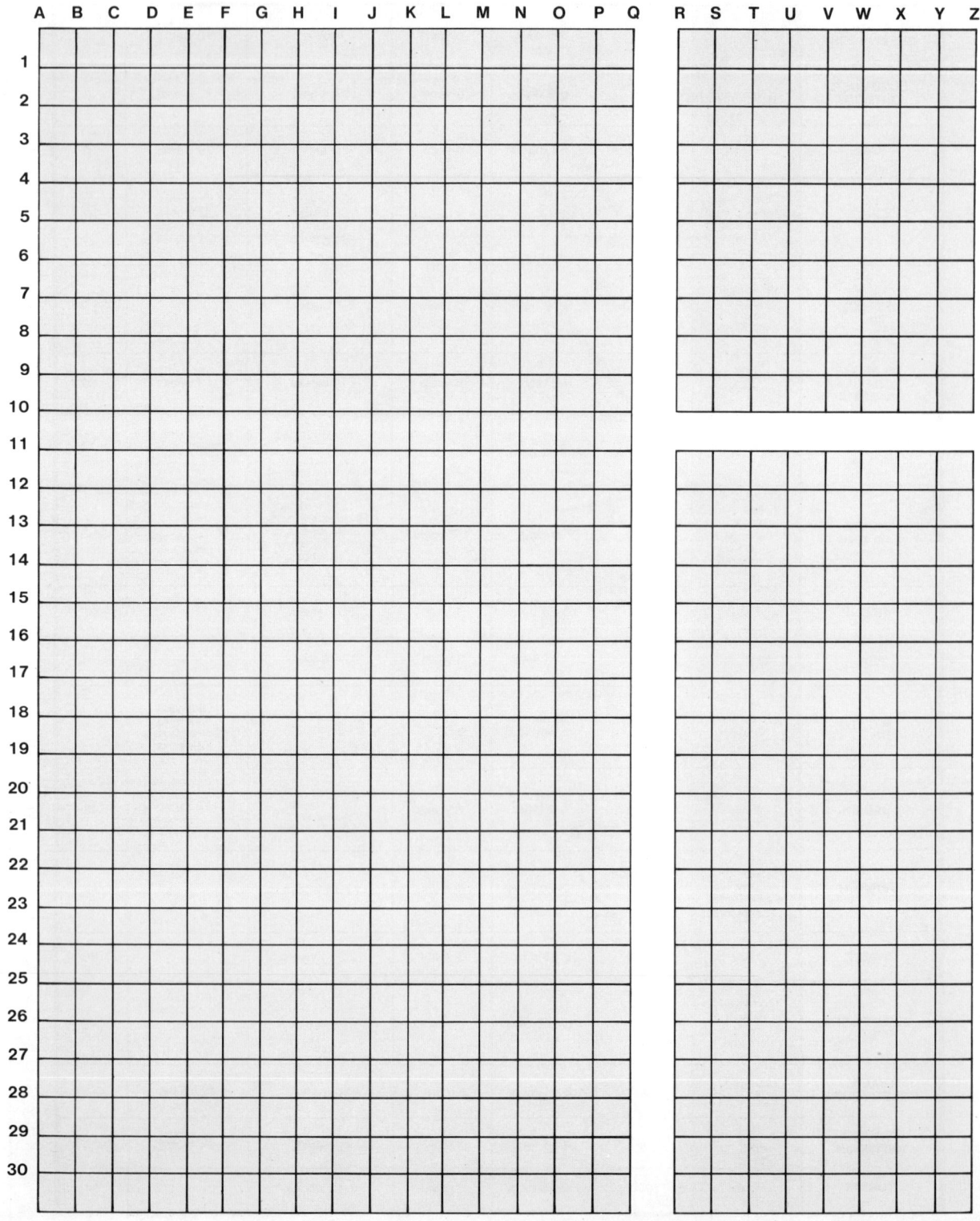

CHAPTER 2
VEGETABLES A~Z

VARIETIES These are not necessarily the "best" varieties — they have been chosen on the basis of their popularity in catalogues, shops and stores

TYPES Basic groups into which the varieties are divided

YIELD The yield which can be expected under average growing conditions

U.K. RECORD Nearly all of the records listed were achieved in the *Garden News/Phostrogen Giant Fruit & Vegetable Competition* 1960–1987

BEETROOT

An easy vegetable which will grow in any reasonable soil. Rather slow to start, but growth is rapid once the seedlings are through. The secret is to avoid any check to growth and to pull the roots before they are large. There are 3 types — the popular globe, the less common cylindrical and the exhibitor's only long. 'Seeds' of standard varieties are corky fruits containing several true seeds. Monogerm varieties produce one seedling per seed.

Harvesting

Pull out roots of globe varieties as required. Twist off (do not cut) leaves. Roots grown for storage should be lifted in October. Shake off soil and discard damaged roots. Place the roots between layers of dry peat in a box and store in a shed. The crop will keep until March.

When the seedlings are about 1 in. high, thin out to leave a single plant at each station. Protection against birds may be necessary. The ground must be kept weed-free. Dryness leads to woodiness — a sudden return to wet conditions leads to splitting. To avoid problems water moderately every fortnight during dry spells.

Pull up alternate plants when roots reach golf-ball size — use for cooking. Leave the remainder to reach maturity.

Varieties

- **BOLTARDY:** Widely available — the usual choice for early sowing. Deep red flesh
- **MONODET:** A monogerm variety — crimson-fleshed and free from rings
- **MONOPOLY:** A monogerm variety — noted for its flavour and resistance to woodiness
- **DETROIT-LITTLE BALL:** A favourite choice for late sowing. Produces 'baby' beets for pickling
- **DETROIT-CRIMSON GLOBE:** The standard choice for later planting — an old favourite
- **DETROIT-NEW GLOBE:** A good choice for exhibiting. Uniform shape, ring-free flesh
- **BURPEE'S GOLDEN:** The skin is orange, and the yellow flesh does not bleed when cut
- **ALBINA VEREDUNA:** The most popular white variety. Leaves can be cooked as greens
- **CYLINDRA:** An oval beet with excellent keeping qualities. Deep red flesh
- **FORONO:** Full-grown roots are an ideal size — 7 in. long and 2 in. across
- **CHELTENHAM GREEN TOP:** The most popular and highly recommended Long variety
- **CHELTENHAM MONO:** A monogerm variety — recommended for showing and winter storage
- **SPRINTER**

	Shape & colour	Bolt resistant	Variety grown	Yield, flavour & notes for next year	Expected yield	U.K. record
		YES				
		YES				
		YES				
		NO				
		NO				
		NO	✓	*Same trouble as last year — the plants ran to seed. The roots were rather woody. Will try Sprinter next year!*	Globe varieties: 18 lb from a 10 ft row / Long varieties: 23 lb from a 10 ft row	Weight: 29 lb (var. Unknown, Kent 1964)
		NO				
		NO				
		NO				
		NO				
		NO				
		NO				
		YES	✓			

* Variety which will not readily run to seed in poor growing conditions

Calendar

Very early crop which will be ready in late May or June, sow a bolt-resistant variety under cloches or in a frame in early March.
Main sowing period begins outdoors in mid April. A second sowing of globe varieties in mid May will provide a regular supply of tender roots.
For sowing for winter storage, sow in late May or June. Roots from earlier sowings may be too large. Lifting time in October.
For an autumn crop sow Detroit-Little Ball in July.

	JAN	FEB	MAR	APR	MAY	JUN	JUL	AUG	SEP	OCT	NOV	DEC
Recommended Sowing Time												
Actual Sowing Dates				4								
Expected Lifting Time												
Actual Lifting Dates									21	10		

For key to symbols see page 7

CALENDAR

- Most popular time for sowing or planting outdoors
- Less usual time for sowing or planting outdoors. The earlier panel generally refers to S. England
- Recommended time for sowing outdoors under cloches or in a cold frame
- Recommended time for sowing indoors under glass
- Recommended time for transplanting seedlings raised under glass
- Recommended time for transplanting seedlings raised under glass. Cover with cloches
- Recommended time for transplanting seedlings raised under glass into pots/bags in the greenhouse
- Most popular time for harvesting
- Less usual time for harvesting

Write in the name of an unlisted variety which you are growing or propose to grow in the garden. The fact that a variety is not listed means that it is not offered by many suppliers – it does not necessarily mean that it is a poor choice

Mark the variety you are growing with a red tick. Use a pencil to tick a variety which you propose to try in the future

Note down your views on performance. In case of a poor showing check in *The Vegetable Expert* to see if you are doing something wrong. It may be time to try a new variety

4 June — the date seed was sown this year

21 September — the date the first roots were lifted for kitchen use

10 October — the date the roots were lifted for storage

ARTICHOKE, GLOBE

Seed Sowing

Raising plants from seed is possible but not advisable. Sow thinly in drills which are 1 in. deep and 1 ft apart. Thin the seedlings — they should be about 9 in. apart in the rows. Plant out in the following spring.

Planting

Plant firmly.
Remove tips of leaves.
Water in thoroughly

36 in. — 36 in. — 2 in.

This vegetable requires a permanent plot — it is more at home in the herbaceous border than in the vegetable plot. It is tall (3–4 ft high) and thistle-like — the arching silvery leaves provide an attractive foil for the bright floral display. It is a fussy plant in many ways, requiring good soil, regular watering, liberal manuring and frost protection in winter. Globe artichokes are usually grown from offsets (rooted suckers) rather than seed. These offsets are taken from either high-yielding plants in the garden or are bought from a garden centre. Roots must be attached and the ideal height is 9 in.

Good drainage is essential — it is a waste of time to grow this crop in heavy clay. Dig the soil in autumn and incorporate compost or well-rotted manure.

Plant as shown above — keep the plants well watered until established. Apply a mulch in May.

During the summer months hoe regularly and apply a liquid fertilizer at fortnightly intervals. Water thoroughly when the weather is dry. Keep watch for aphids and slugs — treat at the first signs of attack.

In late autumn cut down the stems and cover the crowns with bracken, leaves, straw or bark chips. Remove this protective covering in April.

Harvesting

A few small heads will begin to form in the first year — cut off immediately and discard. Cropping begins in the season after planting — the ball-like heads are removed for boiling just before the fleshy scales open. Remove the terminal bud ('kinghead') first, leaving 2–3 in. of stem attached. Feed the plants after this initial cropping — later in the season remove and cook the smaller secondary heads.

Varieties

Variety	Variety grown	Yield, flavour & notes for next year	Expected yield
GREEN GLOBE: The variety you are most likely to find in the seed catalogues. Large, green heads with a good flavour			10–12 heads per mature plant
PURPLE GLOBE: You will have to search for this variety. Hardier than its green relative, but the flavour is inferior			
VERT DE LAON: This one is bought as offsets for planting rather than grown from seed. Compact plants — excellent flavour			
CAMUS DE BRETAGNE: The heads are large and the flavour is good, but it is a rarity. Not suitable for northern counties			
VIOLETTA DI CHIOGGIA: A purple-headed variety to raise from seed for the herbaceous border. Rogue out green-headed plants			

Calendar

Do not plant too many — just 2 or 3 plants will generally provide enough heads for your family.

April is the best month for sowing seeds and for planting offsets.

The plants will not last forever — plant rooted offsets each spring so that mature specimens can be disposed of after a few years.

	JAN	FEB	MAR	APR	MAY	JUN	JUL	AUG	SEP	OCT	NOV	DEC
Recommended Sowing Time			▓	▓								
Actual Sowing Dates												
Recommended Planting Time				▓								
Actual Planting Dates												
Expected Cutting Time							▓	▓	▓	▓		
Actual Cutting Dates												

For key to symbols — see page 7

ASPARAGUS

Seed Sowing

Raising plants from seed is possible, but buying crowns from a garden centre or mail order company is much more popular. Sow seed thinly in drills which are 1 in. deep and 1 ft apart. Thin the seedlings when they are 3 in. tall — they should be about 6 in. apart in the rows. Plant out in the following spring.

Planting

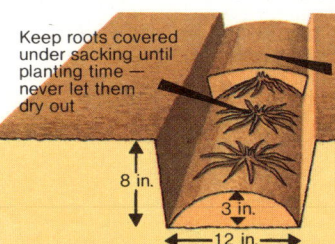

Keep roots covered under sacking until planting time — never let them dry out

Cover crowns with 2 in. of sifted soil immediately after spreading out roots. Fill in trench gradually as plants grow — bed should be level by autumn

Pick a sunny spot sheltered from strong winds. Dig the soil in autumn and incorporate a liberal amount of compost or well-rotted manure. Remove the roots of all perennial weeds during soil preparation.

Plant as shown above — these days you can buy asparagus plants in peat blocks and these are simply planted with a trowel and covered with about 2 in. of soil. Keep the beds weed-free and well watered during dry weather. In summer remove berries before they fall to the ground and in autumn cut down the ferny stems once they have turned yellow. The stumps should be 1–2 in. above the surface.

In subsequent years make a ridge of soil with a draw hoe over each row before the spears appear in spring.

VEGETABLES A–Z

There are two things you will need to grow asparagus successfully — patience and free-draining soil. Patience because you will have to wait until the second year after planting before cutting your first spears — free-draining soil because the fleshy roots soon rot when waterlogged. There are lots of old wives' tales concerning this crop, but in fact you don't need wide spacing, heavy annual dressings of manure nor a regular sprinkling of salt. Thorough soil preparation and careful planting are essential and your reward is a bed of a luxury vegetable which should stay productive for 10–20 years. Asparagus is nearly always raised from rooted plants ('crowns') rather than from seed.

Harvesting

Do not cut any spears in the year of planting nor in the following year. Cutting can begin in the second year after planting. As soon as the spears reach a height of 4–5 in. they should be severed about 3 in. below the soil surface. Use a long serrated kitchen knife. Cut every day if necessary. In early or mid June you must stop cutting so that the spears can develop into the ferny stems which build up the food reserves for next year's crop.

Varieties

	Sex of plants	Variety grown	Yield, flavour & notes for next year	Expected yield
CONNOVERS COLOSSAL: Still the most popular variety, available as seed or crowns. Thick-stalked, crops early and is excellent for freezing	M & F			20–25 spears per mature plant
MARTHA WASHINGTON: A long-established U.S. variety which produces long spears in early June. Rust-resistant and reliable	M & F			
LARAC: A new variety from France which shows great promise. Spears appear early in the season and yields are very high. Good flavour	M & F			
SUTTON'S PERFECTION: A sturdy, well-established variety which is bought as crowns rather than seed	M & F			
LUCULLUS: A new variety which is claimed to give twice the yield of older types. Spears are long and straight	M			

M & F Plants may be male or female
M All-male — male plants are stronger than female ones

Calendar

Use 1-year-old crowns. You can buy 2- or 3-year-old crowns but they can be temperamental.

Plant crowns in early April if the soil is in good condition — delay for a couple of weeks if the weather is cold and wet. Trenches should be dug about 3 ft apart.

Harvesting of the mature crop takes place over a 6–8 week period. To ensure the maximum harvest period, plant a mixed bed containing an early variety such as Connovers Colossal with a later variety such as Martha Washington.

	JAN	FEB	MAR	APR	MAY	JUN	JUL	AUG	SEP	OCT	NOV	DEC
Recommended Sowing Time												
Actual Sowing Dates												
Recommended Planting Time												
Actual Planting Dates												
Expected Cutting Time												
Actual Cutting Dates												

For key to symbols — see page 7

BEAN, BROAD

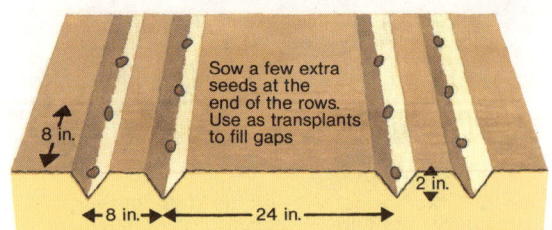

Sow a few extra seeds at the end of the rows. Use as transplants to fill gaps

8 in. — 8 in. — 24 in. — 2 in.

Nearly any soil can produce an adequate crop, although the ideal soil is rich and free-draining. Few vegetables are easier to grow, and these are the first garden beans to grace your table. Picking can begin as early as the end of May if you have pampered the crop, but even the maincrop sown in the ordinary way in early April will be ready for harvest in July.

Hoe regularly to keep down weeds when the plants are small. Watering will not be needed at this stage, but you will have to water copiously in dry weather when the pods are swelling.

Support is necessary for tall-growing varieties. Place a stout cane at each corner of the double row and then stretch twine between these canes.

Pinch off the top 3 in. of stem as soon as the first pods start to form. This will ensure an earlier crop and also provide some degree of blackfly control. This serious pest must be kept down, so spray with Long-last if attacks persist.

Harvesting

Do not leave the pods to reach their maximum size — the beans inside will be tough. Begin picking when the first pods are 2–3 in. long — cook them whole.

The time to pick for shelling is when the beans have begun to show through the pod but before the scar on each shelled bean has become discoloured. Remove the pod with a sharp downward twist.

Types

LONGPOD varieties (L)

The long, narrow pods hang downwards, reaching 15 in. or more in length. There are 8–10 kidney-shaped beans within each pod — both green and white varieties are available. This is the best group for hardiness, early cropping, exhibiting and top yields.

WINDSOR varieties (W)

The pods are shorter and broader than those of the main group — the Longpods. There are 4–7 round beans within each pod — both green and white varieties are available. This is the best group for flavour. They are not suitable for autumn sowing and they take longer to mature than Longpods.

DWARF varieties (D)

The dwarf, freely-branching bushes grow about 12–18 in. high, making them the ideal choice where tall growth is not required or the site is exposed. These are the broad beans to choose for growing under cloches.

Calendar

There are several ways of growing a crop which will be ready for picking in June. November sowing (Aquadulce or The Sutton) will provide beans in early June, but there can be serious losses in a severe winter. Only attempt autumn sowing if your plot is sheltered, free-draining and located in a mild area. It is a better plan to sow under cloches in February.

Maincrop sowings begin in March and then at monthly intervals until the end of May to provide beans throughout the summer.

	JAN	FEB	MAR	APR	MAY	JUN	JUL	AUG	SEP	OCT	NOV	DEC
Recommended Sowing Time		↕	■	■	■						■	
Actual Sowing Dates												
Expected Picking Time						■	■	■	■			
Actual Picking Dates												

For key to symbols — see page 7

Varieties

Name	Type	Bean colour	Variety grown	Yield, flavour & notes for next year	Expected yield	U.K. record
AQUADULCE: This is the standard variety for autumn sowing. Tall, prolific and very hardy. A good choice for freezing	L	white			20 lb from a 10 ft double row	Length: 23⅜ in. (var. *Own Seed*, Roxburgh 1963)
IMPERIAL GREEN LONGPOD: A popular variety for many years — tall, high-yielding with extra-long pods. Now rivalled by Relon	L	green				
RELON: Vigorous and reliable. Pods over 20 in. with 10–11 beans have been claimed. Good for freezing and showing	L	green				
IMPERIAL WHITE LONGPOD: An old favourite with a good reputation for high yields and medals at shows. Now rivalled by Hylon	L	white				
HYLON: One of the newer white-bean varieties which produces longer pods than its rivals. Highly recommended for exhibition and freezing	L	white				
BUNYARD'S EXHIBITION: Still in many catalogues although it's not the biggest nor longest nor tastiest. Just thoroughly reliable	L	white				
MASTERPIECE LONGPOD: A widely available variety with fine-flavoured green beans. Sow in February or March — crops early	L	green				
EXPRESS: Well named — it is one of the fastest maturing of all broad beans. Sow in early spring for a midsummer crop	L	pale green				
RED EPICURE: Not easy to find, but quite different from any other. Beans turn yellow when cooked — flavour quite distinctive	L	red				
DREADNOUGHT: A new Longpod which is recommended for exhibiting as the pods are well-shaped and extraordinarily long	L	green				
JUBILEE HYSOR: A white bean which has begun to appear in a number of catalogues. The beans are closely packed in the pod	L	white				
WITKIEM MAJOR: Claimed in the catalogues that it crops as early as the autumn-sown varieties and gives higher yields	L	green				
COLOSSAL: A good culinary variety — the beans are plump and fine-flavoured. Also recommended for exhibition — pods are long and well-shaped	L	white				
GREEN WINDSOR: Heavy-cropping and perhaps the best-tasting broad bean — but it is now hard to find. It is the parent of many other varieties	W	green				
WHITE WINDSOR: The white-seeded counterpart to Green Windsor. Look for its offsprings such as Imperial White Windsor	W	white				
THE SUTTON: The most popular of the Dwarf varieties — much praise has been heaped on it. Can be sown March–June or November	D	white				
BONNY LAD: Not much to choose between this variety and The Sutton, but it does grow rather taller (15–18 in. compared to 12 in.). Pods 5 in. long	D	white				
BRUNETTE: A new addition to the Dwarf group. The 4–5 in. pods are thin-walled and bear unusually small beans. Good for freezing	D	white				

L Longpod variety
W Windsor variety
D Dwarf variety

VEGETABLES A–Z

BEAN, FRENCH

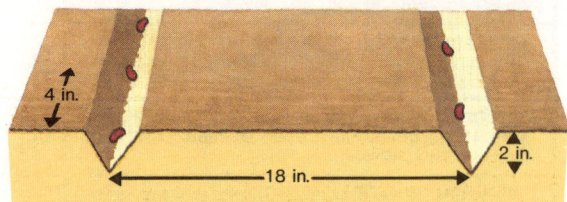

The french bean is a half hardy annual which cannot stand frost. Do not plant before the recommended time — seed will rot in cold and wet soil. If space is short grow them in the flower garden — the bushy plants bear white, pink or red flowers and varieties are available with brightly-coloured pods. An easy crop, provided the site is not heavy clay and is reasonably sunny.

Hoe regularly to keep down weeds when the plants are small. Support the plants with short twigs or pea sticks. Use poles, netting or twiggy branches for climbing varieties.

Spraying the flowers is not necessary to ensure that they will set properly. Moisture at the roots, however, is essential to ensure maximum pod development and a long cropping period. Water copiously and regularly if the weather turns dry during or after the flowering period.

Slugs can be a problem, especially with seedlings, and aphids often attack the plants in summer. Treat at the first signs of trouble. Halo blight can be a problem in a wet season — brown leaf spots with a yellow halo. Unfortunately there is no cure.

Harvesting

A pod is ready for picking if it snaps easily when bent but before the tell-tale bulges of maturity are present. Pick several times a week if necessary — you can expect to continue cropping for 5–7 weeks.

Take care not to loosen the plant when harvesting — hold the stems when tugging away the pods, or use a pair of scissors.

Types

Most french beans are **Bush** varieties, growing as compact branching plants 12–18 in. high. There are a few **Climbing** varieties which will clamber up a support to a height of 5 ft or more. The usual pod colour is green, but you can also buy yellow and purple varieties — there is even a striped one for the novelty seeker. The coloured pod has a practical advantage — the pods can be easily seen at picking time.

FLAT-POD varieties (F)

Before the War these varieties dominated the catalogues. They are the 'English' varieties — flat, rather wide and often with a tendency to become stringy as they mature. You will find the old favourites here, but there are some new stringless varieties such as Limelight.

PENCIL-POD varieties (P)

The catalogues are now dominated by these 'Continental' varieties — round and generally stringless. Small pods are usually cooked whole.

French beans are nearly always eaten in the fresh green pod state — the 'haricot vert' of the French. With some varieties (Chevrier Vert is the notable example) the fresh bean ('flageolet') can be removed from the pods and cooked, or dried ('haricot') for cooking later.

Calendar

	JAN	FEB	MAR	APR	MAY	JUN	JUL	AUG	SEP	OCT	NOV	DEC
Recommended Sowing Time												
Actual Sowing Dates												
Expected Picking Time												
Actual Picking Dates												

For an early crop sow a quick-maturing variety in early May. If you want to pick beans before the end of June then you will have to grow the plants under cloches. Put the cloches in position in early March and sow the seeds in the soil beneath them in early or mid April. Remove the cloches in late May.

The maincrop is sown during May. Successional sowings up to the end of June will provide pods until early October.

For a late autumn crop sow in July and cover the plants with cloches in mid September.

For key to symbols — see page 7

Varieties

	Type	Pod colour	Variety grown	Yield, flavour & notes for next year	Expected yield
THE PRINCE: The most popular variety — you will find it in nearly all the catalogues. Dwarf-growing — pick pods when young. Good for exhibiting	F/B				
MASTERPIECE: Another popular variety — suitable for early sowing and growing under cloches. Pods are long and straight. A prolific french bean	F/B				
CANADIAN WONDER: Once a favourite Flat-pod but it is no longer in the popular catalogues. A heavy cropper, but it fell out of favour	F/B				
LIMELIGHT: The thick pods are broad and stringless. It is claimed to be one of the earliest french beans, and the flavour is sweet	F/B				
BORLOTTO: A real novelty. Both the young pods and the beans are pale green with bright red stripes and blotches	F/B				
GARRAFAL ORO: A climbing variety — this one produces 9 in. long Flat-pods. Prolific and early-maturing — the flavour is distinctive	F/C				
TENDERGREEN: The most popular Pencil-pod variety. It has many good points — stringless, early, prolific and recommended for freezing	P/B				Bush varieties: 8 lb from a 10 ft row Climbing varieties: 12 lb from a 10 ft row
LOCH NESS: A stringless variety with an upright rather than branching growth habit. Withstands colder conditions than most varieties	P/B				
PROS-GITANA: A truly continental bean — round, narrow and stringless. The juicy pods are short — freeze them whole to retain flavour	P/B				
RADAR: Another very slender bean — pick pods at 4 in. stage and cook whole. It is a heavy-cropping variety with a good flavour	P/B				
REMUS: Something different — the pods are borne well above the leaves. This makes picking easier and keeps the pods cleaner	P/B				
DAISY: Similar catalogue description to Remus — slender round pods are carried well above the foliage. Good for freezing	P/B				
CHEVRIER VERT: The most popular haricot variety — eat as green beans, flageolet or haricot beans (see page 12)	P/B				
KINGHORN WAX: A yellow stringless bean renowned for its flavour. The pods are about 6 in. long and the flesh is creamy yellow	P/B				
MONT D'OR: Like Kinghorn Wax, a yellow 6 in. pod with a waxy texture and fine flavour. Usually cooked whole — the beans are black	P/B				
ROYAL BURGUNDY: A small plant bearing straight purple pods which turn green when cooked. Crops well even in dry weather	P/B				
BLUE LAKE: The most popular climbing variety, its 5 ft stems producing a plentiful supply of white-seeded pods. Suitable for drying	P/C				
PURPLE PODDED CLIMBING: The most popular purple climbing (5 ft) variety. The round pods are fleshy and turn green when cooked	P/C				

F Flat-pod variety
P Pencil-pod variety
B Bush variety
C Climbing variety

VEGETABLES A-Z

BEAN, RUNNER

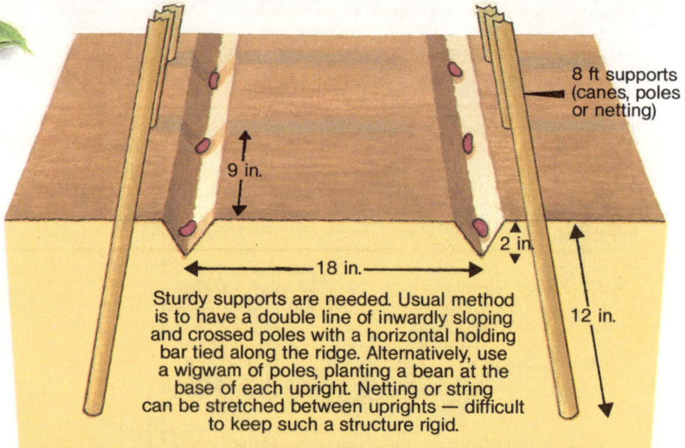

The runner bean or scarlet runner is a rewarding but not really an easy crop to grow. Thorough ground preparation is required in winter and weekly watering is necessary in dry weather once the pods have begun to form. Picking every other day is essential, but the abundance of produce makes all this work worthwhile. White-flowered varieties set more readily than the red ones.

Sturdy supports are needed. Usual method is to have a double line of inwardly sloping and crossed poles with a horizontal holding bar tied along the ridge. Alternatively, use a wigwam of poles, planting a bean at the base of each upright. Netting or string can be stretched between uprights — difficult to keep such a structure rigid.

Tie the young plants to the supports and hoe regularly to keep down weeds. Protect from slugs and water regularly in dry weather once the pods have formed. Misting will not help fruit set but occasional liquid feeding during the cropping season will increase the yield. Pinch out growing points once the tops of the supports have been reached.

Harvesting

Pick regularly once the pods have reached a decent size (6–8 in.) but before the beans inside have started to swell. Removing all the pods at this stage will allow cropping to continue for about 8 weeks.

This means that you will have to harvest every couple of days — leaving even a small number of pods to ripen will stop production.

Types

STICK varieties (S)

Nearly all runner beans will grow 8–10 ft high and bear pods which can reach 10–20 in. long. They are grown on tall supports and the usual flower colour is red. There is a bi-colour variety (Painted Lady) and the white and pink varieties are self-pollinating.

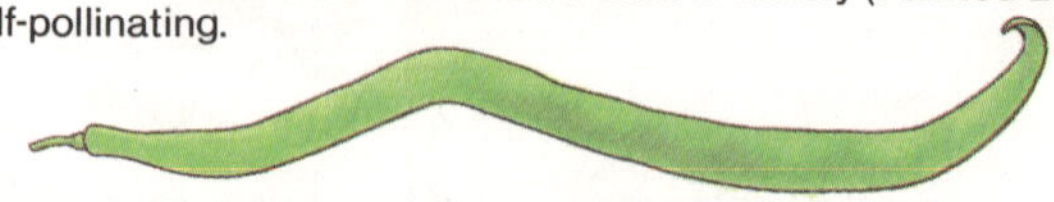

GROUND varieties (G)

A few Stick varieties can be sown 2 ft apart and grown as bushy plants by pinching out the growing point of the main stems when they are about 12 in. high. Side shoots are pinched out and the stems are supported by short twigs. The pods appear earlier than on climbing plants but there are disadvantages. The cropping period is short and pods are often curled and soiled.

DWARF varieties (D)

True Dwarfs are available — the plants grow 12–18 in. high and the pods are 6–8 in. long. They should be grown about 6 in. apart in rows 2 ft wide. A good choice where space is limited, but yields cannot compare with their climbing relatives.

Calendar

The standard method of growing runner beans is to sow the seeds outdoors when the danger of frost is past — the end of May in the south or early June in the north. Always sow a few extra seeds at the ends of the rows — use the seedlings as transplants to fill gaps.

A second sowing in June in mild areas will ensure an October crop.

Runner beans are often raised by planting out seedlings when the danger of frost is past. These seedlings are either shop-bought (make sure that they have been properly hardened-off) or raised at home from seeds sown under glass in late April. This planting-out method is strongly recommended for the colder areas of the country.

	JAN	FEB	MAR	APR	MAY	JUN	JUL	AUG	SEP	OCT	NOV	DEC
Recommended Sowing Time (outdoors)												
Actual Sowing Dates (outdoors)												
Recommended Sowing Time (under glass)												
Actual Sowing Dates (under glass)												
Expected Picking Time												
Actual Picking Dates												

For key to symbols — see page 7

Varieties

Description	Type	Stringless	Variety grown	Yield, flavour & notes for next year	Expected yield	U.K. record
PRIZEWINNER: Pods are medium length — cropping is heavy and the flavour is good. An old favourite, but the pods can be stringy	S	NO			60 lb from a 10 ft double row	Length: 39½ in. (var. *Own Seed*, Salop 1986)
PRIZEWINNER STRINGLESS: A new one for the fans of Prizewinner. All the same features are there, but it is stringless	S	YES				
ENORMA: The improved form of Prizewinner — produces the slender shape and size of pod which wins prizes at the horticultural show	S	NO				
STREAMLINE: A well-established variety like Prizewinner — reliable and prolific. The problem is the stringiness of older pods	S	NO				
ACHIEVEMENT: Still popular for table use and exhibiting. The pods are long and it has proved its reliability over the years	S	NO				
RED KNIGHT: You will find this one in lots of catalogues. A stringless red-flowering variety, and that is unusual. Pods are long	S	YES				
MERGOLES: White flowers and white seeds — an excellent runner bean for kitchen use. Pods are produced over a long period	S	YES				
DESIREE: Similar to Mergoles — white flowers are followed by long and slender pods. Produces well even in dry weather — highly recommended	S	YES				
BUTLER: A vigorous variety which crops over a very long period. Pods are fleshy and often over 12 in. long — a good choice	S	YES				
POLESTAR: A new scarlet-flowered runner — claimed to crop very heavily. The flowers set very easily and the season starts early	S	YES				
PAINTED LADY: Recommended as a climber to cover unsightly walls or fences — the flowers are white and red. Recommended for freezing	S	NO				
BOKKIE: A new red-flowered variety which is claimed to produce pods earlier than any other scarlet runner. Pods 9–10 in. long	S	NO				
SUNSET: Different in a couple of ways — the blooms are pale pink and the self-fertilizing flowers produce a very early crop	S or G	NO				
KELVEDON MARVEL: Straight pods are produced very freely. An early cropper with rather short pods which grows well as a Ground bean	S or G	NO				
SCARLET EMPEROR: A popular choice — similar to Kelvedon Marvel in many ways. Cropping starts early etc, but pods are longer	S or G	NO				
GULLIVER: Plants are only 15–18 in. high, but the curved and smooth pods are 7 in. long. Early and prolific	D	YES				
PICKWICK: Another modern Dwarf which does not need support. Height 12 in. — crops early and for a long period if picked regularly	D	YES				
HAMMONDS DWARF: The original non-climbing runner bean. It is red-flowered and early maturing. Grows about 18 in. tall	D	NO				

S *Stick variety*
G *Ground variety*
D *Dwarf variety*

VEGETABLES A-Z

BEET, LEAF

Leaf beets are close relatives of the ordinary beetroot, but they are grown for their leaves and not the roots. Both spinach beet and swiss chard are cooked and used like spinach — with swiss chard the leaves are used as a spinach substitute and the fleshy stalks are cooked like asparagus. If your soil is sandy or infertile you should choose a leaf beet variety. Spinach grown under such conditions will either quickly run to seed or produce bitter leaves — leaf beets are much easier to grow.

Any reasonable soil in sun or light shade will do for leaf beet. Incorporate some compost or well-rotted manure during autumn digging.

Thin the seedlings to 1 ft apart when they are large enough to handle. Hoe regularly to keep the land weed-free. Bolting is most unlikely, but promptly remove any seed-heads which may appear. Slugs can be a problem in late spring — sprinkle Slug Pellets around the plants.

Water at fortnightly intervals during dry spells. Mulching will help to conserve moisture.

Harvesting

Twist off (do not cut) outer leaves when they are large enough for cooking — do not wait until maximum size is reached. Harvest carefully and regularly — leave the central foliage to develop for later pickings. Do not disturb the roots. Avoid storage if possible. If you must keep it, place in a polythene bag in the refrigerator for up to 2 days.

Varieties

Spinach beet bears leaves which are darker, larger and fleshier than ordinary spinach. It is not a popular vegetable although the seeds appear in all the catalogues. Even less popular are the **swiss chard** varieties. They have thick and prominent midribs — the effect is attractive enough for the plant to be grown in the flower border. If the soil is heavy and low in organic matter choose a swiss chard variety rather than spinach beet.

	Type	Variety grown	Yield, flavour & notes for next year	Expected yield
SPINACH BEET: Other names — perpetual spinach, leafy beet. Contains less oxalic acid than ordinary spinach — taste is less earthy	SB			7 lb from a 10 ft row
SWISS CHARD: Other names — seakale beet, silver beet. Grows about 1½ ft high. White and fleshy midribs are 3–4 in. across	SC			
RUBY CHARD: Other name — rhubarb chard. Similar in growth habit to swiss chard but the stalks are thinner and red	SC			
RAINBOW CHARD: The leaf beet if you want something different — the stems are red, purple, yellow or white	SC			
LUCULLUS: Savoy-like leaves and broad midribs — the most prolific and hardiest of swiss chard varieties	SC			
FORDHOOK GIANT: The midribs are creamy white and exceptionally wide. In the textbooks but not in the catalogues	SC			

SB *Spinach beet variety*
SC *Swiss chard variety*

Calendar

	JAN	FEB	MAR	APR	MAY	JUN	JUL	AUG	SEP	OCT	NOV	DEC
Recommended Sowing Time												
Actual Sowing Dates												
Expected Picking Time												
Actual Picking Dates												

A spring sowing will be ready for harvesting to begin in late July or early August — continue picking throughout summer and autumn. In late autumn cover the plants with cloches or straw — cropping can then continue throughout the winter months and into spring and early summer.

For key to symbols — see page 7

page 17

BEETROOT

An easy vegetable which will grow in any reasonable soil. Rather slow to start, but growth is rapid once the seedlings are through. The secret is to avoid any check to growth and to pull the roots before they are large. There are 3 types — the popular globe, the less common cylindrical and the exhibitor-only long. 'Seeds' of standard varieties are corky fruits containing several true seeds. Monogerm varieties produce one seedling per seed.

When the seedlings are about 1 in. high, thin out to leave a single plant at each station. Protection against birds may be necessary. The ground must be kept weed-free.
Dryness leads to woodiness — a sudden return to wet conditions leads to splitting. To avoid problems water moderately every fortnight during dry spells.
Pull up alternate plants when roots reach golf-ball size — use for cooking. Leave the remainder to reach maturity.

Harvesting

Pull out roots of globe varieties as required. Twist off (do not cut) leaves. Roots grown for storage should be lifted in October. Shake off soil and discard damaged roots. Place the roots between layers of dry peat in a box and store in a shed. The crop will keep until March.

VEGETABLES A–Z

Varieties

	Shape & colour	Bolt ★ resistant	Variety grown	Yield, flavour & notes for next year	Expected yield	U.K. record
BOLTARDY: Widely available — the usual choice for early sowing. Deep red flesh		YES			Globe varieties: 10 lb from a 10 ft row / Cylindrical varieties: 14 lb from a 10 ft row / Long varieties: 18 lb from a 10 ft row	Weight: 29 lb 0 oz (var. *Unknown*, Kent 1964)
MONODET: A monogerm variety — crimson-fleshed and free from rings		YES				
MONOPOLY: A monogerm variety — noted for its flavour and resistance to woodiness		YES				
DETROIT-LITTLE BALL: A favourite choice for late sowing. Produces 'baby' beets for pickling		NO				
DETROIT-CRIMSON GLOBE: The standard choice for later planting — an old favourite		NO				
DETROIT-NEW GLOBE: A good choice for exhibiting. Uniform shape, ring-free flesh		NO				
BURPEE'S GOLDEN: The skin is orange, and the yellow flesh does not bleed when cut		NO				
ALBINA VEREDUNA: The most popular white variety. Leaves can be cooked as greens		NO				
CYLINDRA: An oval beet with excellent keeping qualities. Deep red flesh		NO				
FORONO: Full-grown roots are an ideal size — 7 in. long and 2 in. across		NO				
CHELTENHAM GREEN TOP: The most popular and highly recommended long variety		NO				
CHELTENHAM MONO: A monogerm variety — recommended for showing and winter storage		YES				

★ Variety which will not readily run to seed in poor growing conditions

Calendar

	JAN	FEB	MAR	APR	MAY	JUN	JUL	AUG	SEP	OCT	NOV	DEC
Recommended Sowing Time												
Actual Sowing Dates												
Expected Lifting Time												
Actual Lifting Dates												

For a very early crop which will be ready in late May or early June, sow a bolt-resistant variety under cloches or in a frame in early March.

The main sowing period begins outdoors in mid April. A second sowing of globe varieties in mid May will provide a regular supply of tender roots.

When growing for winter storage sow in late May or June — the roots from earlier sowings may be too coarse at lifting time in October.

For a late autumn crop sow Detroit-Little Ball in July.

For key to symbols — see page 7

BROCCOLI

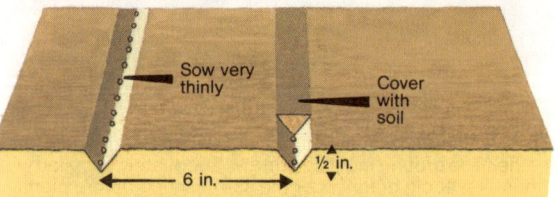

The frozen spears from the supermarket are really calabrese or green broccoli — the garden grown variety is usually purple sprouting broccoli. There are four types to choose from for growing at home — all are sown in spring and planted in summer. The purple type is the hardiest and most popular — the white type is less popular and produces small cauliflower-like spears. The harvest time is February-March (early varieties) or April-May (late varieties). Green types of broccoli are cropped earlier (August-October) and should be more widely grown. Finally there is perennial broccoli which produces heads every year.

Thin seedlings to 3 in. apart in the rows. When 3 in. high transplant to permanent quarters — set seedlings 1 in. deeper than in seed bed. Leave 1½ ft between purple and white varieties — 1 ft between green varieties.

Hoe around transplants and protect from birds. Water in dry weather and apply a mulch. Watch for pests. As winter approaches draw up soil around stems and support if necessary. Netting may be needed to keep pigeons away.

Harvesting

Cut when the spears are well formed but before the flower buds have opened. Cut or snap off the central spear first. Side shoots will appear and these should be picked regularly — never let them flower. The spears should be about 4–6 in. long and cropping lasts for about 6 weeks.

Varieties

Variety	Colour	Expected yield
EARLY PURPLE SPROUTING: The most popular variety — hardy and prolific	purple	
LATE PURPLE SPROUTING: Robust like other purples — plants grow about 3 ft tall	purple	
EARLY WHITE SPROUTING: The variety to grow for spears in March	white	
LATE WHITE SPROUTING: Used to extend the broccoli season — crops in April-May	white	1½ lb per plant
CORVET (F₁): Popular — large central head followed by secondary spears	green	
EXPRESS CORONA (F₁): Central head followed by secondary spears — ready in August	green	
GREEN DUKE (F₁): A low growing variety which starts to crop in September	green	
GREEN COMET (F₁): An early cropper — just one large central head is produced	green	
GREEN SPROUTING: Old variety — taller than Corvet. Produces abundant secondary spears	green	
NINE STAR PERENNIAL: Produces several small cauliflower heads each year. Plant 3 ft apart	green	

Calendar

The date you can expect to start cutting depends on the variety and the weather. Early Purple Sprouting will be ready for its first picking in January if the winter is mild but mid spring is the peak harvesting period for the purple and white varieties.

The green varieties will be ready for cutting in autumn — choose Express Corona or Green Comet if you are in a hurry. Cropping will extend into winter if prolonged frosts do not occur.

	JAN	FEB	MAR	APR	MAY	JUN	JUL	AUG	SEP	OCT	NOV	DEC
Recommended Sowing Time				■	■							
Actual Sowing Dates												
Recommended Planting Time						■	■					
Actual Planting Dates												
Expected Cutting Time		EARLY vars.		LATE vars.				GREEN vars.				
Actual Cutting Dates												

For key to symbols — see page 7

BRUSSELS SPROUTS

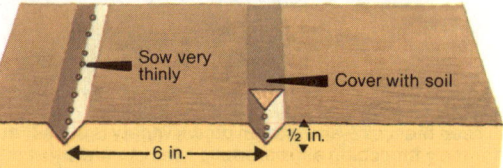

Loose, open sprouts are caused by bad gardening, not bad weather. The ground must be firm and adequately supplied with humus. Never dig or fork over the soil in spring before planting — merely tread down, rake lightly and remove surface rubbish. You can begin picking in September and finish in March if you grow both early and late varieties. These days F_1 hybrids are usually chosen — the growth habit is compact and a large number of uniform and long-lasting buttons crowd the stems. The old favourite Standard varieties have none of this uniformity nor high quality and the buttons quickly blow if not picked promptly.

Thin seedlings to 3 in. apart in the rows. When 4–6 in. high transplant to permanent quarters — set seedlings with their lowest leaves just above the soil surface. Plant firmly. Leave 1½ ft (compact F_1 hybrid varieties) — 2½ ft (Standard varieties) between plants.

Hoe around plants and protect from birds. Water in dry weather. Watch out for caterpillars and aphids — spray if necessary. As autumn approaches earth-up around the stems and stake tall varieties before the high winds of winter arrive.

Harvesting

Begin picking when the sprouts ('buttons') at the base are the size of a walnut. Tug sharply downwards or use a sharp knife. Work steadily upwards at each cropping session — remove only a few sprouts at any one time from each individual stem. Cropping lasts for about 8 weeks.

Varieties

Variety	Type	Colour	Variety grown	Yield, flavour & notes for next year	Expected yield
PEER GYNT: The favourite brussels sprout. Early medium-sized sprouts September-December	F_1	green			
CITADEL: Later than Peer Gynt — reaches its peak on Christmas Day. Dark green	F_1	green			
FORTRESS: Another late variety (January-March). Buttons dark green and very firm	F_1	green			
ROGER: A good choice if you want large sprouts early in the season	F_1	green			2 lb per plant
WIDGEON: Fine flavour — a mid-season variety (November-February). Good disease resistance	F_1	green			
ORMAVON: Interesting variety which produces a cabbage-like head as well as sprouts	F_1	green			
RAMPART: A late variety — holds its sprouts for a long time without blowing	F_1	green			
TROIKA: Lacks uniformity of F_1 hybrids but gives same quality and yield	T	green			
BEDFORD FILLBASKET: Heavy-cropping old favourite (October-January). Sprouts are large	S	green			
RUBINE: The red one (October-January). Yields are low — flavour is excellent	S	red			
ROODNERF: November-January. Sprouts remain sound and can be picked over a long period	S	green			

F_1 F_1 hybrid variety
T Three-way cross variety
S Standard variety

Calendar

Sow an early variety outdoors in mid March and plant out in mid May to provide sprouts during October and November. To obtain September sprouts, sow the seeds under cloches in early March and plant out in early May.

For a later crop which will produce sprouts between December and March, sow a late variety in April and plant out in June.

	JAN	FEB	MAR	APR	MAY	JUN	JUL	AUG	SEP	OCT	NOV	DEC
Recommended Sowing Time			▓	▓								
Actual Sowing Dates												
Recommended Planting Time					▓	▓						
Actual Planting Dates												
Expected Picking Time	▓	▓	▓						▓	▓	▓	▓
Actual Picking Dates												

For key to symbols — see page 7

VEGETABLES A-Z

page 19

CABBAGE

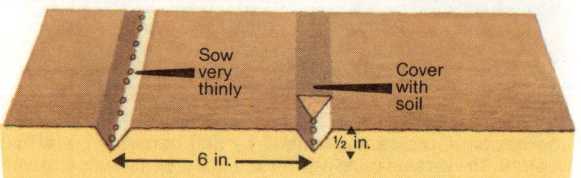

If you have the space and inclination it is quite possible to have heads ready for cutting all year round. Well-consolidated soil is essential, so leave several months between digging and planting. Lime the soil if it is acid. Before planting tread down gently, rake lightly and remove surface rubbish. Nearly all of the host of varieties in the catalogues fall neatly into one of the three major groups — spring, summer or winter cabbage. The season refers to the time of harvesting, not planting. Savoys are a special type of winter cabbage — red cabbage is grown like other summer varieties.

Harvesting

Thin out spring cabbage in March and use the thinnings as spring greens. Cabbages are harvested by cutting close to ground level with a sharp knife. With spring and summer varieties cut a ½ in. deep cross into the stumps — a secondary crop of small cabbages will appear.

Thin seedlings to 3 in. apart in the rows. When there are 5 or 6 leaves transplant to permanent quarters — dip roots in Calomel Dust if club root is feared. Plant firmly. Leave 1–1½ ft between plants — 4 in. apart in 1 ft rows for spring cabbage.

Hoe around plants and protect from birds. Water in dry weather. Apply a liquid feed as the heads mature and keep watch for pests. In autumn earth-up the stems of spring cabbage.

SPRING CABBAGE
These cabbages are planted in the autumn to provide tender spring greens (collards) in early spring and larger mature heads later in the season. They are generally conical in shape and smaller than the summer and winter varieties.

SUMMER CABBAGE
These cabbages are generally ball-shaped with a few conical exceptions. The normal pattern is to sow outdoors in April, transplant in May and cut in August or September. For June cabbages sow an early variety under cloches in early March.

WINTER CABBAGE
These cabbages are generally ball-headed or drum-headed. They are green or white and suitable for immediate cooking. The white varieties are also used for Coleslaw and can be stored for months. Sow in May and transplant in July.

SAVOY
These cabbages are easily recognised by their crisp and puckered dark green leaves. They are grown as winter cabbages but there is a wider harvesting span — there are varieties which mature in September and others as late as March.

For key to symbols — see page 7

Varieties

Variety	Type	Variety grown	Yield, flavour & notes for next year	Expected yield	U.K. record
DURHAM EARLY: Popular, especially as a source of spring greens. Dark green with conical heads. Early, but does not heart up well	SPR			Spring varieties: ¾–1 lb per plant Summer varieties: 1½ lb per plant Winter and savoy varieties: 2½–3 lb per plant	Weight: Cabbage (Green) 118 lb 0 oz (var. *Tex*, Wiltshire 1987) Cabbage (Savoy) 38 lb 0 oz (var. *Unknown*, Notts 1966)
APRIL: Another early variety which is both compact and reliable. The pointed dark green heads are rather small. Few outer leaves	SPR				
SPRING HERO: Something different — a ball-headed spring cabbage. This F_1 hybrid crops early, but sow in August and not July	SPR				
PIXIE: A new one which is now highly recommended. Use as spring greens or leave to form firm hearts in May	SPR				
OFFENHAM 2·FLOWER OF SPRING: No worries about the weather with this one — it is very hardy. Large solid heads in April-May	SPR				
WHEELER'S IMPERIAL: An old variety, but still widely grown. The dark green, solid heads are small and pointed. Cut in April	SPR				
GREYHOUND: A popular variety for early sowing. The solid pointed hearts mature quickly and they are ready for cutting in July	SUM				
HISPI: This F_1 hybrid is even earlier than the old favourite Greyhound. Same shape, but can be cut in June	SUM				
HAWKE: A dark green F_1 hybrid which is ready in September-October. The round heads are medium-sized. Stands well for many weeks	SUM				
PRIMO: The favourite ball-headed summer cabbage — compact and very firm. Ready in July or August — medium-sized	SUM				
MINICOLE: A popular F_1 hybrid. The small oval heads are produced in early autumn — will stand for 2-3 months without splitting	SUM				
RED DRUMHEAD (NIGGERHEAD): The favourite red cabbage — firm and compact hearts which are dark red in colour. Can be stored until March	SUM				
CELTIC: An F_1 hybrid of a savoy and winter white cabbage. Blue-green and ball-headed — ready for cutting from November	WIN				
CHRISTMAS DRUMHEAD: Earlier than Celtic — the compact heads can be harvested in October. A reliable variety renowned for its hardiness	WIN				
JANUARY KING: The hardiest of all — savoy-type but without crinkled leaves. Tinged with red — ready between November and January	WIN				
HOLLAND LATE WINTER: The favourite white cabbage for Coleslaw and storage. Heads are large and firm, and are ready in November-December	WIN				
JUPITER: An F_1 hybrid which is dark green on the outside and white inside. Can be stored like a white variety	WIN				
BEST OF ALL: The most popular early savoy — ready in September or October. Drum-headed, solid and very large	SAV				
ORMSKIRK LATE: This old favourite does not reach cutting size until February-March. Heads are large and dark green — leaves are deeply crinkled	SAV				

SPR *Spring variety*
SUM *Summer variety*
WIN *Winter variety*
SAV *Savoy variety*

VEGETABLES A-Z

CAPSICUM

The capsicum is a relative of the tomato and requires similar growing conditions — it is really a greenhouse crop but can be grown outdoors in the south if you are lucky with the weather. The varieties which are becoming popular are the large sweet peppers — their small and fiery relatives known as chilli peppers are much less popular. In the greenhouse the plants are grown in 9 in. pots or planted in growing bags — the stems grow about 3 ft tall. Outdoor plants are shorter — they need well-drained, fertile soil in a sunny sheltered spot. Capsicum is a difficult crop — regular watering, feeding, spraying and staking are needed.

Seed Sowing

Raise seedlings under glass at 60°–70°F. Sow 2 seeds in a compost-filled peat pot — remove the weaker seedling. For pot culture it is necessary to repot in several stages until the plants are ready to be moved to their permanent site under glass. Harden off before planting outdoors.

Planting

Cover the soil with cloches for 2 weeks before planting. Replace the cloches after planting.

Mist plants regularly to keep down red spider mite and to encourage fruit set. Some form of support is necessary — attach stems to stakes or horizontal wires. Pinching out the growing point is not recommended.

Water regularly but do not keep the compost or soil sodden. Add Bio Tomato Food with each watering once the fruits have begun to swell.

Harvesting

The fruits are ready for picking when the peppers are green, plump and glossy. Cut as required. You may prefer to eat them at the coloured stage rather than when they are green. You can leave them on the plant to ripen — this is practical under glass but it is usually preferable to cut the fruit and let them ripen on the windowsill when the crop is grown outdoors.

Varieties

Variety	Colour	Variety grown	Yield, flavour & notes for next year	Expected yield
CANAPE: A popular variety — one to choose for outdoor cultivation. Prolific and early, but the fruits are rather small. Mild and sweet	red			6–10 peppers per plant
GYPSY: An F₁ hybrid recommended for cold greenhouse culture. Early, like Canape, and a heavy cropper. Slightly tapered rather than block-shaped	red/green			
YELLOW LANTERN: One of the capsicums which turn yellow when ripe. Other examples are Gold Star, Luteus and Top Banana	yellow			
TRITON: A compact (1 ft) variety for growing in 6 in. pots. The 4 in. fruits are highly ornamental as well as flavourful	red			
WAXLIGHTS: A mixture of fruits which turn white, red, violet or yellow when ripe. An ornamental plant, but fruits are as edible as plainer varieties	white/violet/yellow			

Calendar

Prick out seedlings into 3 in. pots when 3 leaves have formed.

A straightforward greenhouse crop. Plant seedlings in pots or growing bags (3 to a bag) in late April (heated glass) or mid May (unheated glass).

A risky crop outdoors — a site against a south wall in a mild district is necessary.

	JAN	FEB	MAR	APR	MAY	JUN	JUL	AUG	SEP	OCT	NOV	DEC
Recommended Sowing & Planting Time (outdoors)			■			🌱						
Actual Sowing & Planting Dates (outdoors)												
Recommended Sowing & Planting Time (greenhouse)		■	■	🏠	🏠							
Actual Sowing & Planting Dates (greenhouse)												
Expected Picking Time												
Actual Picking Dates												

For key to symbols — see page 7

page 23

CARROT

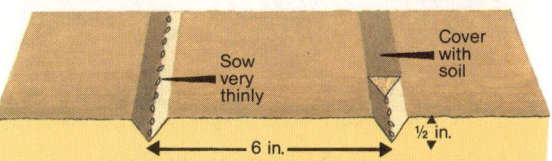

Carrots are not a difficult crop if the soil is good and the dreaded carrot fly is kept away. If your soil is stony and heavy, grow a Short-rooted variety — these carrots are golf-ball round or finger long. They are the first to be sown and mature quickly. The Intermediate-rooted varieties are the best all-rounders for the average garden. Some are pulled for immediate use and the rest are left to mature for winter storage. The Long-rooted varieties are the tapered giants of the show bench. Spectacular, but not really suitable for general garden use.

Do not add fresh manure or compost to the soil before sowing. Sow seed very thinly to reduce the need for thinning to a minimum. Thin seedlings to 2–3 in. apart when they are large enough to handle. Protect against carrot fly by thinning in the evening and burning or burying the removed seedlings.

Pull out weeds by hand — avoid hoeing if possible. Water during periods of drought in order to keep the ground moist — a downpour on dry soil may cause root splitting.

Harvesting

Pull up small carrots as required from June onwards. Ease them out with a fork if the soil is hard. October is the time to lift maincrop carrots for storage. Remove surface dirt and place between layers of sand or dry peat.

Varieties

Variety	Type	Variety grown	Yield, flavour & notes for next year	Expected yield	U.K. record
AMSTERDAM FORCING: One of the earliest — little care and excellent for freezing	S			Early carrots: 8 lb from a 10 ft row. Maincrop carrots: 10 lb from a 10 ft row	Weight: 10 lb 4 oz (var. *Flak*, Wiltshire 1984)
EARLY NANTES: Like Amsterdam Forcing — early, tender and good for freezing	S				
EARLY FRENCH FRAME: Round roots up to 2 in. across. Good in shallow soils	S				
CHAMPION SCARLET HORN: An early variety recommended for sowing under cloches	S				
KUNDULUS: A good carrot for bad soils or small plots. Almost ball-shaped	S				
CHANTENEY RED CORED: A very popular choice — smooth-skinned and deep orange	I				
AUTUMN KING: Unusually long for an intermediate. Extremely hardy and healthy	I				
NANTES TIP TOP: Cylindrical roots about 6 in. long. Core-free and sweet-flavoured	I				
JAMES SCARLET INTERMEDIATE: An old favourite renowned for all-round performance	I				
MOKUM: An F_1 hybrid which produces roots up to 9 in. long. Quick maturing	I				
NEW RED INTERMEDIATE: Despite the name, one of the longest of all carrots	L				
ST VALERY: Long and finely tapered — a popular choice for exhibition	L				

S   Short-rooted variety
I   Intermediate-rooted variety
L   Long-rooted variety

Calendar

	JAN	FEB	MAR	APR	MAY	JUN	JUL	AUG	SEP	OCT	NOV	DEC
Recommended Sowing Time			✓	■	■	■		■				
Actual Sowing Dates												
Expected Lifting Time						■	■	■	■	■		
Actual Lifting Dates												

For a very early crop which will be ready in June, sow a Short-rooted variety under cloches or in a cold frame in early March.

For an early crop which will be ready in July, sow a Short-rooted variety in a sheltered spot in late March or early April.

For maincrop carrots sow Intermediate- or Long-rooted varieties between mid April and early June for lifting in September and October.

For a tender crop in November and December, sow a Short-rooted variety in August and cover with cloches from October.

For key to symbols — see page 7

VEGETABLES A-Z

CAULIFLOWER

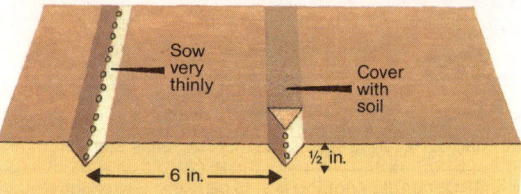

Cauliflower is more difficult to grow than cabbage. It needs deep and rich soil which must be well-consolidated — never dig in spring prior to planting. You must make sure there is no check to growth, which calls for regular watering in dry weather. Failure to provide the right conditions will result in the production of tiny 'button' heads. Varieties are available to produce heads nearly all year round, but avoid the Roscoff types which are not hardy in most parts of the country. You can grow a giant, such as Flora Blanca, or a compact type like Alpha-Polaris.

Thin seedlings to 3 in. apart in the rows. When there are 5 or 6 leaves transplant to permanent quarters — dip roots in Calomel Dust if club root is feared. Plant firmly. Leave 2 ft between summer and autumn varieties, 2½ ft between winter varieties.

Hoe around plants and protect from birds. Water in dry weather and feed occasionally. With summer types bend a few leaves over the curd to protect it from the sun — with winter types a few leaves broken over the curd will protect the head from frost and snow.

Harvesting

Do not wait for all the heads to mature — cut some while they are still quite small. Harvest in the morning when the heads still have dew on them — in frosty weather wait until midday. Cut all cauliflowers before the florets start to separate.

Types

SUMMER CAULIFLOWER
These cauliflowers mature during the summer months from seed sown in a cold frame in September, in a greenhouse or on the windowsill in January or outdoors in April. They are compact plants — you can choose an early variety, such as Snowball, which will produce heads in June or July, or you can grow a later-maturing type like All the Year Round which will be ready for cutting in August from an outdoor sowing.

AUTUMN CAULIFLOWER
These cauliflowers mature during the autumn months and are of two quite different types. There are the large and vigorous varieties such as Autumn Giant and Flora Blanca, and there are the more compact Australian varieties such as Barrier Reef and Canberra.

WINTER CAULIFLOWER
'Winter cauliflower' is the technically incorrect name for the group of varieties listed on the next page. The standard types mature in spring, not winter, and they are really heading broccoli. Although less delicately-flavoured than true cauliflowers the popular varieties of winter cauliflower are easier to grow.

Calendar

Summer varieties: In late March or early April transplant seedlings which have been raised under glass from a January sowing to provide a June-July crop. Or sow outdoors in early April and transplant in June for cropping in August-September.

Autumn varieties: Sow outdoors between mid April and mid May and transplant in late June.

Winter varieties: Sow outdoors in May and transplant in late July.

	JAN	FEB	MAR	APR	MAY	JUN	JUL	AUG	SEP	OCT	NOV	DEC
Recommended Sowing Time				■	■							
Actual Sowing Dates												
Recommended Planting Time						■	■					
Actual Planting Dates												
Expected Cutting Time			WINTER vars.	WINTER vars.	WINTER vars.		SUMMER vars.	SUMMER vars.		AUTUMN vars.	AUTUMN vars.	
Actual Cutting Dates												

For key to symbols — see page 7

Varieties

Variety	Type	Variety grown	Yield, flavour & notes for next year	Expected yield	U.K. record
ALL THE YEAR ROUND: For many years the No.1 choice. White, large curds excellent for cooking, freezing and exhibiting	SUM			Summer varieties: ½–1 lb per plant Autumn varieties: 1–2 lb per plant Winter varieties: ½–1 lb per plant	Weight: 52 lb 12 oz (var. Metropole, W. Sussex 1966)
DOK-ELGON: A successor to All the Year Round for showing. The heads are large, maturing in late summer. Reliable and recommended	SUM				
ALPHA-POLARIS: An early variety for June-July cropping. Resists premature heading better than most. Several 'Alpha' strains available — Climax etc	SUM				
SNOWBALL: Another early cauliflower — very popular. The heads are tight but not large. For large heads choose the F_1 hybrid Snow Crown	SUM				
ANDES: A very compact variety for cutting in August-September. Sow under glass in February for July cropping. Cooking quality is excellent	SUM				
PREDOMINANT: Not in many catalogues but worth looking for. Sow in permanent quarters and thin to 6 in. for mini-cauliflowers	SUM				
DOMINANT: A robust variety which matures in July. The heads are large and firm — the quality is good. Recommended for freezing	SUM				
ELBY: An exciting newcomer which thrives in poorer soils better than standard varieties. Heads are large and closely packed. Well worth trying	SUM				
AUTUMN GIANT: The dominant autumn type before the Australian varieties appeared. Still useful if you want large heads in early winter	AUT				
FLORA BLANCA: Another old favourite — an excellent choice for exhibition. The extra-large heads are ready in September-October. Pure white curd	AUT				
MILL REEF: One of the compact Australian varieties with pure white, solid heads. Ready from October onwards. Reliable, uniform and closely packed	AUT				
BARRIER REEF: Another Australian variety for cutting from late October. The compact growth habit and good head quality of this group are present	AUT				
CANBERRA: A popular Australian cauliflower which matures in November. The curd is well protected by the broad leaves	AUT				
ENGLISH WINTER: Once the basic hardy variety for March-June cropping. Strains include St George (April), Late Queen (May) and Late June (June)	WIN				
WALCHEREN WINTER: Dutch variety now taking over from English Winter. Heads are claimed to be superior in quality. Several strains are available	WIN				
PURPLE CAPE: Purple heads instead of the usual white. Large and hardy — ready for cutting in March. Cook leaves as well as curd	WIN				
ANGERS NO.1: An early variety (January-February) but typical of the group of frost-sensitive types which occur in some catalogues	WIN				
ASMER SNOWCAP: A medium-sized variety to choose if you want to cut winter cauliflowers at the start of the season in early March	WIN				

SUM *Summer variety*
AUT *Autumn variety*
WIN *Winter variety*

VEGETABLES A-Z

CELERIAC

Seed Sowing

Sow two seeds in a compost-filled peat pot — remove the weaker seedling. Harden off the seedlings before planting outdoors.

Planting

A popular vegetable in parts of Europe but it is not often seen in British shops or allotments. The knobbly, swollen stem-bases known as 'roots' are about 4–5 in. across and are peeled, cubed and boiled like turnips. The flavour is distinctly celery-like, hence the common name 'turnip-rooted celery'. This is not a vegetable for all gardens. Try some before deciding to grow it as the flavour does not appeal to everyone. It is also not an easy plant to grow — rich, moisture-retentive soil is required and so is regular watering. Slugs, carrot fly and celery fly can be a nuisance.

Plant firmly with the stem-base at ground level. Do not bury the crown. Water in after planting.

Hoe regularly and feed occasionally. Water thoroughly if dry spells occur during the growing season — a mulch in early summer will help to conserve moisture.

Remove side shoots — from midsummer onwards cut off the lower leaves so as to expose the crown. In late September draw soil around the swollen stem-bases.

Harvesting

There is no point in lifting the roots before they reach maximum size — neither flavour nor texture deteriorate with age. Lifting begins in October — use a garden fork. In most areas there is no need to store the roots — just cover the plants with peat and lift as required until spring. In heavy soils lift all roots in November and store in damp peat.

Varieties

Variety	Description
MARBLE BALL	The best-known variety but found in few catalogues. Medium-sized, globular and strongly flavoured
TELLUS	Quick-growing with a smoother skin than most varieties. Flesh remains white when cooked
GIANT PRAGUE	This variety is noted for the large size of the roots. Flavour is stronger than average
SNOW WHITE	An early celeriac with the whitest flesh of all. Roots are large and round
GLOBUS	Matures rather late, but the weight is larger than average and the roots store well
JOSE	Earliness is the main claim to fame of this variety. Roots are uniform in shape
IRAM	This medium-sized celeriac seems to have disappeared from all the popular catalogues. Similar to Marble Ball
CLAUDIA	The smoothest of all the celeriacs. Easy to prepare for cooking, but suppliers are rare

Expected yield: 7 lb from a 10 ft row

Calendar

Celeriac is not hardy — seedlings have to be raised from seeds sown under glass in early spring.

Seedlings are planted in their permanent site outdoors when all danger of frost is past.

	JAN	FEB	MAR	APR	MAY	JUN	JUL	AUG	SEP	OCT	NOV	DEC
Recommended Sowing Time			●●									
Actual Sowing Dates												
Recommended Planting Time					🌱	🌱						
Actual Planting Dates												
Expected Lifting Time										▪	▪	▪
Actual Lifting Dates												

For key to symbols — see page 7

page 27

CELERY

Seed Sowing

Sow seeds under glass. Prepare the trench in April. Seedlings are ready for transplanting when there are 5–6 leaves — harden off before planting outdoors.

Planting

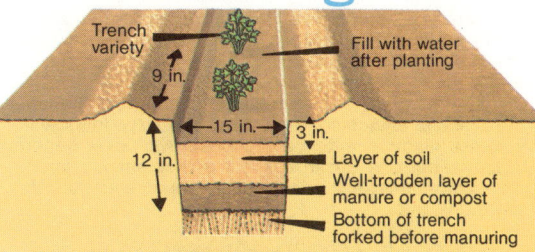

Plant Self-blanching varieties 9 in. apart in a block, not in rows. Water copiously and feed regularly during the summer months.

Begin blanching Trench varieties in early August by covering stems with newspaper or cardboard and then filling the trench with soil. In late August mound moist soil against the stems. In September heap up again so that only the green tops are showing. Do not let soil fall into the hearts.

The Trench varieties involve a lot of effort — the planting site must be carefully prepared and the crop must be earthed-up at intervals to lengthen and remove the stringiness from the stems. Nowadays there are Self-blanching varieties to make the task of celery growing easier. Trenching and earthing-up are not necessary, but there are drawbacks. The flavour is less pronounced and the crop cannot be left in the ground once the frosts arrive. Furthermore Self-blanching celery is not an 'easy' crop — regular watering and feeding and humus-rich soil are still required.

Harvesting

Lift white Trenching varieties from October to Christmas — pink and red ones in January. Start at one end of the row — replace soil to protect remaining plants. Lift Self-blanching varieties as required from August until the frosts arrive. Do not pull — use a trowel to avoid disturbing neighbouring plants.

Varieties

	Type	Colour	Variety grown	Yield, flavour & notes for next year	Expected yield	U.K. record
GIANT WHITE: The standard white-stalked celery — needs good growing conditions. Various strains (e.g Solid White) are sold	T				12 lb from a 10 ft row	Weight: 35 lb 8 oz (var. Suttons Red, Merseyside 1973)
GIANT PINK: Similar to Giant White, but sticks are tinged with pink. Hardy — matures in late winter	T					
GIANT RED: Very hardy variety — the sticks are greenish purple, turning pink when blanched. Heads are large and firm	T					
GOLDEN SELF-BLANCHING: The standard yellow-stalked celery — low-growing and ready for cropping from August onwards	SB					
LATHOM SELF-BLANCHING: An alternative to Golden Self-Blanching if you want a yellow variety — less likely to bolt	SB					
CELEBRITY: Similar to Lathom Self-Blanching in earliness and bolt-resistance, but the sticks are longer	SB					
IVORY TOWER: Tall for a Self-blanching variety — the sticks are pale green, crisp and stringless. Ready for cropping in early autumn	SB					

T Trench variety
SB Self-blanching variety

Calendar

Buy celery seedlings for planting in late May–mid June. Or raise your own by sowing seed under heated glass between mid March and early April — make sure that the seedlings do not receive any check to growth and ensure that the plants are properly hardened off before planting.

Self-blanching varieties will be ready for lifting between August and October. The Trench varieties are grown for winter use from October onwards.

	JAN	FEB	MAR	APR	MAY	JUN	JUL	AUG	SEP	OCT	NOV	DEC
Recommended Sowing Time			▮	▮								
Actual Sowing Dates												
Recommended Planting Time					🌱	🌱						
Actual Planting Dates												
Expected Lifting Time	▮	▮						▮	▮	▮	▮	▮
Actual Lifting Dates												

For key to symbols — see page 7

VEGETABLES A-Z

CHICORY

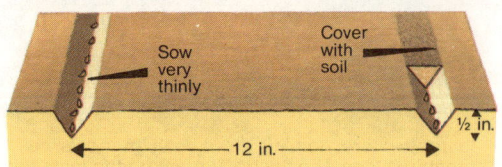

There are two basic types. The Forcing chicories are the more popular, producing plump leafy heads ('chicons') from roots kept in the dark during the winter months. The usual colour is white, but red ones can be forced to produce the red and white leaves served as *radicchio*. The other chicories are the Non-forcing varieties which do not require blanching — they produce large lettuce-like heads which are ready in autumn. Chicons have never become really popular in the U.K. Bitterness is the problem — remember that home-grown ones kept in the dark are much less bitter than shop-bought chicons.

Choose a sunny site. Thin the seedlings to 6 in. (Forcing varieties) or 12 in. (Non-forcing varieties). Hoe to keep down weeds — water in dry weather.
Lift the parsnip-like roots of Forcing chicory in November — discard ones with crowns less than 1 in. across. Cut roots to 6 in. and leaves to 1 in. above the crown — store horizontally in sand. To produce chicons plant 5 roots in a 9 in. pot of peat in November-March. Leave crowns exposed. Cover pot with an empty larger one — block the drainage hole. Keep at 50°–60°F.

Harvesting

Cut chicons after 3–4 weeks forcing — they should be about 6 in. high. Cut just above the crown and then water the compost. Replace the cover — small secondary chicons will be produced. Cut Non-forcing chicory in autumn — use immediately or store in a cool shed.

Varieties

Variety	Type
WITLOOF: Belgian Chicory — the traditional Forcing variety. Needs a soil covering rather than an upturned pot	F
NORMATO: A modern Forcing variety which produces firm chicons. Easier to grow than Witloof	F
ZOOM: An F₁ hybrid Forcing variety which produces compact chicons. Easier to grow than Witloof	F
SUGAR LOAF: The traditional Non-forcing variety. Matures in October — looks rather like a Cos lettuce	NF
CRYSTAL HEAD: One of the newer Non-forcing varieties — others include Winter Fare. Hardier than Sugar Loaf	NF
ROSSA DE VERONA: A ball-headed red-leaved chicory. Treat as a Forcing or Non-forcing variety	F or NF
TREVISO: An upright red-leaved chicory. Treat as a Forcing or Non-forcing variety	F or NF

Expected yield: 6 lb from a 10 ft row

F Forcing variety
NF Non-forcing variety

Calendar

	JAN	FEB	MAR	APR	MAY	JUN	JUL	AUG	SEP	OCT	NOV	DEC
FORCING varieties — Recommended Sowing Time					●	●						
Expected Cutting Time	●	●	●	●								●
NON-FORCING varieties — Recommended Sowing Time						●	●					
Expected Cutting Time										●	●	

For key to symbols — see page 7

COURGETTE

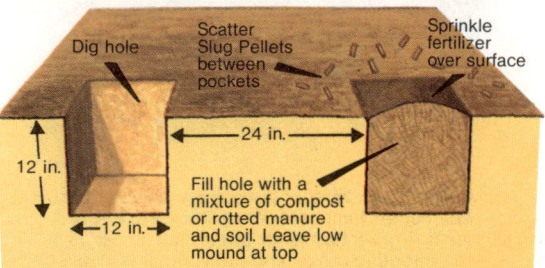

Sow 3 seeds 1 in. deep at the centre of each pocket — cover with a cloche. Remove the 2 weaker seedlings. Plants can be raised indoors, but this method is often less satisfactory. Place a single seed edgeways ½ in. deep in compost — keep at minimum 65°F.

Water copiously around the plants in dry weather — place black polythene or a mulch under the stems before fruit formation. Once the fruits start to swell feed regularly with a liquid fertilizer.

Courgettes are nothing more than marrows cut at an immature stage. The flesh is firmer and the taste superior — in recent years they have taken over from the large watery vegetable marrows. Courgettes are now plentiful in the shops and bountiful in the garden where scores can be obtained from just a few plants. Choose a compact bush variety which is recommended for courgette rather than marrow production. It is essential that you cut all the fruits at the small courgette stage — if you let just a few mature into marrows then production will cease. Blanch for about 2 minutes in boiling water to remove bitterness before serving raw in salads.

Harvesting

Remove the fruits when they are still quite small — 4–5 in. is the ideal size. Do not pull them off the stems — use a sharp knife. Continual cropping is essential.

Varieties

Variety	Type	Colour	Variety grown	Yield, flavour & notes for next year	Expected yield
ZUCCHINI: The most popular courgette variety — dark green fruits borne in profusion. Serve raw or cook as a hot vegetable	S	green			
GOLDEN ZUCCHINI: Until recently the standard yellow courgette. The flesh is creamy and has a good flavour. A late cropper	S	yellow			
GOLD RUSH: The golden-yellow fruits are narrow with creamy-white flesh. Preferred by some to Golden Zucchini because it crops earlier	S	yellow			16 courgettes per plant
GREEN BUSH: One of the favourite all-rounders — cut the small fruits as courgettes and let a few mature into large, striped marrows	F₁	green			
ARISTOCRAT: One of the newer F₁ hybrids. The courgettes are very dark — the plants are vigorous and earlier than average	F₁	green			
AMBASSADOR: A new one — claimed to be very high yielding over a long season. Open growth habit makes picking easier	F₁	green			
EL DORADO: A high-yielding variety with deep orange-yellow courgettes. An early cropper — try it instead of Golden Zucchini	F₁	yellow			

S *Standard variety*
F₁ *F₁ hybrid variety*

Calendar

Sow outdoors in late May or early June. In the Midlands and northern areas cover the seedlings with cloches if you can for a few weeks. The first courgettes will be ready in July.

For an earlier crop sow seeds under glass in late April. Plant out the seedlings in early June when the danger of frost has passed.

	JAN	FEB	MAR	APR	MAY	JUN	JUL	AUG	SEP	OCT	NOV	DEC
Recommended Sowing Time (outdoors)					■	■						
Actual Sowing Dates (outdoors)												
Recommended Sowing Time (under glass)				■	✿							
Actual Sowing Dates (under glass)												
Expected Cutting Time							■	■	■			
Actual Cutting Dates												

For key to symbols — see page 7

CUCUMBER, GREENHOUSE

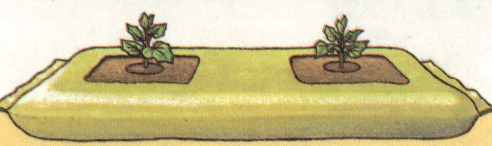

If you want fruits in May or June then growing cucumbers under glass rather than outdoors is necessary. A well-grown specimen of a greenhouse (or frame) cucumber is straight, cylindrical, smooth-skinned and shiny. But it is also a difficult thing to grow. Warmth, high humidity, regular watering and feeding, pest control, regular stopping and so on are all required. Ordinary varieties are the traditional type — long and straight, but male flowers have to be removed or fruit will be bitter. All-female varieties are available.

Sow seed edgeways ½ in. deep in a 3 in. pot. Plant out 1 per pot, 2 per growing bag.

Maintain minimum of 60°F (Ordinary varieties) or 70°F (All-female varieties). Keep compost and air moist — spray floor to maintain high humidity.

Train stems up a wire or cane. Pinch out the tip of each side shoot at 2 leaves beyond a female (swollen base) flower. Remove all male flowers. Feed every 2 weeks once fruits have started to swell.

Harvesting

Cut (do not pull) when the fruit has reached a reasonable size and the sides are parallel. Cropping will cease if you allow cucumbers to mature and turn yellow on the plant.

Varieties

Variety	Type	Expected yield	U.K. record
TELEGRAPH: The most popular Ordinary variety — reliable and still in most catalogues	O	25 cucumbers per plant	Weight: 13 lb 10¾ oz (var. Zeppelin, Kent 1984) Length: 38 in. (var. Unknown, Essex 1983)
BUTCHER'S DISEASE RESISTING: Another old favourite — higher yields but rougher skins than Telegraph	O		
CONQUEROR: A good choice for growing under cool conditions. Fruits are long and smooth	O		
SIGMADEW: An almost white cucumber noted for its flavour and thin skin	O		
PERPINEX: First of the All-females. High yields and freedom from bitterness	F		
PETITA: Small fruits, about 8 in. long, borne in large numbers	F		
ATHENE: Good choice for a cold house. Dark green skin, high-quality flesh	F		
FEMBABY: One for the windowsill — compact plants, small fruits and easy to train	F		
UNIFLORA D: Self-pruning — side shoots grow 6 in. long and then stop	F		
FEMSPOT: For heated houses only — long, bitter-free fruits appear early	F		
BRUNEX: Claimed to be very prolific and tolerant of temperature changes	F		

O Ordinary variety
F All-female variety

Calendar

Sowing should take place in late February or early March for planting in a heated greenhouse or late April for an unheated greenhouse or frame.

Plant out in late March (heated greenhouse) or late May (unheated greenhouse).

	JAN	FEB	MAR	APR	MAY	JUN	JUL	AUG	SEP	OCT	NOV	DEC
Recommended Sowing Time		■	■🏠	🏠■	🏠							
Actual Sowing Dates												
Expected Cutting Time						▨	▨	▨	▨	▨		
Actual Cutting Dates												

For key to symbols — see page 7

CUCUMBER, OUTDOOR

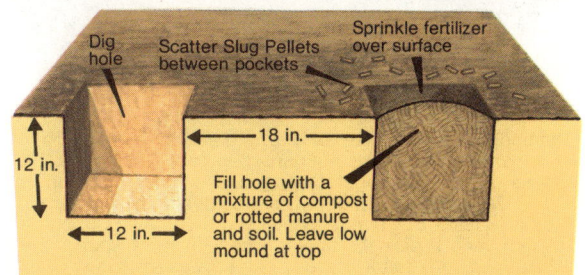

Outdoor (or ridge) cucumbers have developed remarkably in recent years. The Standard ridge varieties do still exist — short, dumpy fruits with warty skins. So do the Gherkin varieties which are even smaller and equally knobbly, but now there are the All-female varieties which are almost seed-free and also the Japanese varieties which are long, smooth and straight like greenhouse cucumbers. Finally there is the small Apple group with round and yellow fruits.

See page 30 for details of seed sowing — keep seeds under glass at 70°–80°F until germinated. Pinch out growing tips when stems have 6–7 leaves — train up netting or leave to trail. Remove non-flowering shoots at the 7th leaf.

Water around plants and mist in dry weather. Place black polythene over the soil before fruit formation. Do not remove male flowers. Feed once the first fruits have started to swell.

Harvesting

Cut before the fruits reach maximum size in order to encourage further fruiting. Most types will be 6–8 in. long. Use a sharp knife — don't tug them. The harvesting period is quite short — the plants are killed by the first frosts.

Varieties

Variety	Type
KING OF THE RIDGE: A long-established and reliable variety — the fruits are almost smooth	SR
BURPEE HYBRID: Vigorous and prolific. The 9 in. cucumbers have smooth, dark green skins	SR
ZEPPELIN: The giant of the group — can be cultivated under glass	SR
PATIO PIK: A popular dwarf — can be grown as a pot plant. Prolific	SR
SWEET SUCCESS: Long fruits which are usually seed- and burp-free	F
CHINESE LONG GREEN: The fruits are smooth-skinned and about 1 ft long	J
KYOTO: Another Japanese variety to rival the cucumbers in the supermarket	J
BURPLESS TASTY GREEN: This is the one to choose — short fruits devoid of bitterness	J
VENLO PICKLING: The most popular Gherkin grown for pickling. Small and warty	G
HOKUS: Earlier and more prolific than Venlo Pickling, say the suppliers	G
CRYSTAL APPLE: Yellow and apple-like — the flesh is crisp and white	A

Expected yield: 10 cucumbers per plant

SR Standard ridge variety   J Japanese variety   A Apple variety
F   All-female variety   G Gherkin variety

Calendar

Sow outdoors in late May or early June. In the Midlands and northern areas cover the seedlings with cloches if you can for a few weeks. Cropping should start in early August.

For an earlier crop sow seeds under glass in late April. Plant out the seedlings in early June when the danger of frost has passed.

For key to symbols — see page 7

KALE

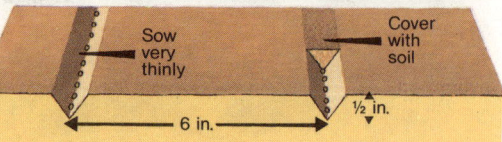

The books sing the praises of kale (or borecole) as a source of winter and spring greens, but gardeners take little notice. It is the hardiest of all vegetables, grows in poor soil and is untroubled by all the dreaded brassica pests. The problem is the bitter taste, but that is avoidable these days. Choose a modern variety, pick the leaves when they are young and tender, and cook them properly. Curly kales are the popular ones, the Plain-leaved varieties are cropped in early spring and rape kale is harvested in March-May. Best of all is the Leaf & spear variety.

Thin seedlings to 3 in. apart — transplant when they are 4–6 in. high. Plant firmly, with the lowest leaves just above the soil surface. Leave 18 in. between the plants.

Treat rape kale varieties differently. Sow where the plants will grow — leave 18 in. between the rows and 18 in. between the plants.

Hoe regularly, firm the plants if necessary and water in dry weather. Earth-up around the stems as autumn approaches — stake tall varieties.

Harvesting

Pick your leaves from the crown of Curly kale varieties from November onwards. In spring gather side shoots when they are 4–5 in. long. Break off or use a sharp knife.

Varieties

Variety	Type	Variety grown	Yield, flavour & notes for next year	Expected yield
DWARF GREEN CURLED: The most popular variety, especially for a small plot. The 1½–2 ft plants do not need staking and the flavour is good	CL			
TALL GREEN CURLED: Less popular than the dwarf version — leaves are dark green and suitable for freezing. Sometimes listed as Tall Scotch Curled	CL			
WESTLAND AUTUMN: A dwarf kale which provides tightly-frilled leaves from November to February. Good choice, but not widely available	CL			2 lb per plant
SPURT: Leaves are dark green and loosely curled — main advantage is that it can be grown without transplanting	CL			
THOUSAND-HEADED KALE: Sometimes praised in the textbooks. It is very hardy and prolific, but you would do better with Pentland Brig	PL			
COTTAGERS: Like all Plain-leaved varieties it is the spring shoots and not the leaves which are eaten. Turns purple in winter	PL			
HUNGRY GAP: A late cropper, like all rape kales. Robust and reliable, producing shoots which are suitable for freezing	RK			
PENTLAND BRIG: Pick young leaves in November, young shoots in early spring and broccoli-like spears in mid spring. Obviously a good choice	LS			

CL Curly-leaved variety RK Rape kale variety
PL Plain-leaved variety LS Leaf & spear variety

Calendar

If you want greens before Christmas, sow a variety of Curly-leaved kale in April. For later cropping sow Leaf & spear or Plain-leaved kale in May. The correct time for transplanting is governed by the height of the seedlings rather than the date.

Thin in stages to leave 18 in. between the plants.

Rape kale is sown in late June. For later management of the crop see details above.

	JAN	FEB	MAR	APR	MAY	JUN	JUL	AUG	SEP	OCT	NOV	DEC
Recommended Sowing Time				■	■	■						
Actual Sowing Dates												
Recommended Planting Time						■	■					
Actual Planting Dates												
Expected Cutting Time	■	■	■	■	■						■	■
Actual Cutting Dates												

For key to symbols — see page 7

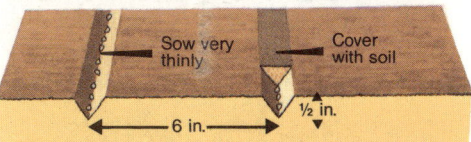

LEEK

Leeks are less demanding than onions and will grow in any reasonable soil. They will withstand the hardest winter, are generally untroubled by pests and diseases and do not demand a high level of fertility. Still, they are not an 'easy' crop — transplanting and earthing-up are required and the land is occupied for a long time. The Early varieties are sown under glass for a September crop or outdoors for an autumn harvest. The Mid-season varieties are the most popular ones with a harvest period from December to January. The Late varieties mature between February and April.

Thin seedlings to 1½ in. apart — transplant when they are 8 in. high and as thick as a pencil. Trim off root ends and leaf tips, then set out 6 in. apart in rows 12 in. apart. Use a dibber — drop plant into a 6 in. deep hole and fill with water to settle roots.

Hoe and water as necessary. Earth-up during the season, drawing up soil around the stems at intervals so as to increase the length of white stem. Do not let soil fall between leaves. Finish in late October.

Harvesting

Begin lifting when the leeks are quite small — flavour decreases as size increases. Do not pull the plants out of the ground — use a fork. Lift during the winter as required.

Varieties

Variety	Type	Variety grown	Yield, flavour & notes for next year	Expected yield	U.K. record
LYON-PRIZETAKER: A favourite exhibition variety over the years. Mild flavoured and long-stemmed	E			10 lb from a 10 ft row	Weight: 9 lb 6 oz (var. Unknown, Merseyside 1973)
PANCHO: A new Early — long, straight stems which can stand until mid winter	E				
EARLY MARKET: A strain of Autumn Mammoth noted for its earliness — not winter-hardy	E				
MUSSELBURGH: The favourite home-grown leek — hardy, reliable and thick-stemmed	M				
SNOWSTAR: Similar to Musselburgh in general appearance, but a better choice for showing	M				
ARGENTA: Thick stems 1½ in. across and grey-green leaves. Tender and mild	M				
KING RICHARD: The stems are significantly longer than the other Mid-season varieties	M				
CATALINA: An outstanding Late variety. Long, very thick and stands well over winter	L				

E Early variety
M Mid-season variety
L Late variety

Calendar

For exhibiting in the autumn sow seed under glass in late January or February and plant outdoors during April.

For ordinary kitchen use sow seed outdoors in spring when the soil is workable and warm enough to permit germination — for all but warm and sheltered areas this means mid March or later. Transplant the seedlings in June.

For an April crop you can sow seed of a Late variety in June and transplant in July.

	JAN	FEB	MAR	APR	MAY	JUN	JUL	AUG	SEP	OCT	NOV	DEC
Recommended Sowing Time			■	■								
Actual Sowing Dates												
Recommended Planting Time						■						
Actual Planting Dates												
Expected Lifting Time	■	■	■	■					■	■	■	■
Actual Lifting Dates												

VEGETABLES A-Z

For key to symbols — see page 7

LETTUCE

Lettuce is grown everywhere. A row or two is sown in spring and again in early summer, the seedlings are thinned and the heads are cut when a heart has formed. The results are often disappointing — plants quickly bolt, leaves are leathery or there is a glut and famine situation. The answer is to sow very short rows every two weeks and to follow the rules — lime if necessary, thin as soon as possible, don't transplant, and water regularly. The cabbage types (Butterhead and Crisphead varieties) dominate the catalogues, but both Cos and Loose-leaf varieties are worth growing.

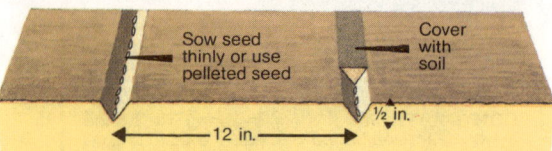

Thin seedlings as soon as the first true leaves appear. Continue thinning until the plants are 12 in. apart – 9 in. for Tom Thumb and Little Gem.

You can try transplanting but lettuce hates to be moved. Wherever possible sow seed where the plants are to mature. Protect seedlings from slugs and birds. Hoe as required.

Water in the morning in dry weather — never in the evening. Keep watch for greenfly and grey mould.

Harvesting

Lettuce is ready for cutting as soon as a firm heart has formed — leaving it will result in the heart growing upwards (bolting). Pull up the whole plant and cut off the root and lower leaves.

Types

LOOSE-LEAF varieties
These varieties do not produce a heart. The leaves are curled and are picked like spinach — a few at a time without cutting the whole plant. Sow seed in April or May.

COS varieties
The Cos or Romaine lettuce is easy to recognise by its upright growth habit and oblong head. The leaves are crisp and the flavour is good. They are generally a little more difficult to grow than the cabbage types and take longer to mature.

CRISPHEAD varieties
The Crispheads produce large hearts of curled and crisp leaves. In general they are more resistant to bolting than the Butterheads, and their popularity is increasing in Britain. They have always been the popular group in the U.S. where the Iceberg type (Crispheads with a solid heart and few outer leaves) are dominant.

BUTTERHEAD varieties
The Butterheads are still the most popular lettuce group. They are quick-maturing and will generally tolerate poorer conditions than the other types. The leaves are soft and smooth-edged — most are summer varieties but a few are hardy lettuces which are used to produce a spring crop and several others are forcing varieties for growing under glass.

Calendar

		JAN	FEB	MAR	APR	MAY	JUN	JUL	AUG	SEP	OCT	NOV	DEC
For a Summer/Autumn Crop Sow outdoors in late March–late July for cutting in June–October. For an earlier crop (mid May–early June) sow under glass in early February and plant out in early March under cloches.	Recommended Sowing Time		■	✿									
	Actual Sowing Dates												
	Expected Cutting Time												
	Actual Cutting Dates												
For an Early Winter Crop Sow a mildew-resistant variety such as Avondefiance or Avoncrisp outdoors in early August. Cover with cloches in late September — close ends with panes of glass. The crop will be ready for cutting in November or December.	Recommended Sowing Time												
	Actual Sowing Dates												
	Expected Cutting Time												
	Actual Cutting Dates												
For a Spring Crop If you live in a mild part of the country, sow a winter-hardy variety such as Valdor or Winter Density outdoors in late August–early September. Thin to 3 in. apart in October — complete thinning to 12 in. spacing in early spring. The crop will be ready in May. For less favoured areas sow in mid October under cloches — harvest in April. Use a winter-hardy or a forcing variety.	Recommended Sowing Time												
	Actual Sowing Dates												
	Expected Cutting Time												
	Actual Cutting Dates												

For key to symbols — see page 7

Varieties

Variety	Type	Variety grown	Yield, flavour & notes for next year	Expected yield
ALL THE YEAR ROUND: A very popular medium-sized variety — pale green and slow to bolt. It can be sown in spring, summer or autumn	B			
AVONDEFIANCE: The dark green heads are mildew-resistant — a good choice for June-August sowing. Slower to bolt than most Butterheads	B			10–20 heads from a 10 ft row
CONTINUITY: Sow this one in spring. The heads are compact and tinged with red — a good choice for sandy soils	B			
BUTTERCRUNCH: The creamy heart of this American variety is unusually hard and crisp for a Butterhead. Stands for a long time without bolting	B			
DOLLY: Highly recommended by the experts — a large Butterhead which has good disease resistance. Good, but not widely available	B			
TOM THUMB: The favourite lettuce for small plots and window boxes, producing tennis-ball heads in summer from a spring sowing	B			
HILDE: A popular choice for sowing under glass in early spring and planting out in March for a May crop	B			
VALDOR: A good winter-hardy variety — Arctic King is another. Sow outdoors in late summer for a spring crop of dark green heads	B			
KWIEK: A reliable greenhouse variety for sowing in October for an early winter crop. Other greenhouse ones are Dandie and May Queen	B			
WEBB'S WONDERFUL: Britain's favourite Crisphead — it's in all the catalogues. Reliable, large-hearted and frilly with tightly-folded heads	C			
LAKELAND: An Iceberg-type of Crisphead which has been bred to be more reliable in Britain than the original Iceberg variety	C			
MARMER: An Iceberg-type of Crisphead for growing under glass. Sow in October in an unheated house and cut in April	C			
SALADIN: Another Iceberg-type — the heads are large and slow to bolt. The flavour is excellent and it is highly recommended	C			
AVONCRISP: Pick this one if you've had problems. It is mildew-resistant, tolerant of root aphid and is not likely to bolt	C			
LITTLE GEM: Compact and regarded by many as the sweetest lettuce. Small, loose heads mature quickly. Good choice for a tiny plot	COS			
LOBJOIT'S GREEN: An old favourite with dark green, self-folding leaves. Large and crisp — the most popular tall Cos	COS			
WINTER DENSITY: The No.1 winter-hardy Cos — sow in August or September for an April crop. Heads are crisp and sweet	COS			
SALAD BOWL: An endive-like plant with leaves which are intricately cut and curled. Pick regularly. A reddish-brown variety is available	LL			

B   *Butterhead variety*
C   *Crisphead variety*
COS   *Cos variety*
LL   *Loose-leaf variety*

MARROW, SQUASH & PUMPKIN

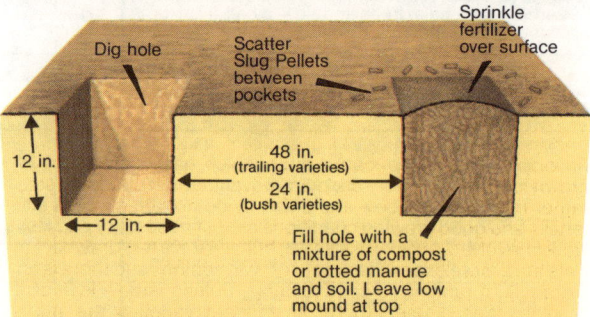

See page 29 for details of seed sowing. Keep the soil moist — water copiously around the plants, not over them. Syringe lightly in dry weather. Pinch out the tips of the main shoots of trailing varieties when they reach 2 ft.

Place black polythene or a mulch around the plants before fruit formation. Once the fruits start to swell feed regularly with a liquid fertilizer. Keep marrows on a tile or sheet of glass.

All these vegetables belong to the gourd family, and only marrow is popular in Britain. In recent years courgettes (immature marrows) have become the most popular member of the group — see page 29. Marrows — large, oblong and striped, are available in both bush and trailing types. Squashes come in a variety of shapes, colours and flavours — excellent alternatives to the ordinary marrow. Summer squashes have soft skin and pale flesh — winter squashes have a hard rind and fibrous orange flesh. Pumpkins are the giants — grown for show in Britain but for other uses in the U.S.

Harvesting

Remove plants for immediate use when they are still quite small — marrows should be 8–10 in. long. They are ready when your thumbnail goes in quite easily at the stalk end of the marrow. Continual cropping is essential. For pumpkins, winter squashes and marrows for winter storage, allow the fruits to mature on the plants and remove before the frosts arrive.

Varieties

	Type	Variety grown	Yield, flavour & notes for next year	Expected yield	U.K. record
LONG GREEN TRAILING: Large and cylindrical with pale stripes. Grow for exhibition	M			4 marrows per plant	Marrow weight: 105 lb 8 oz (var. Long Green, Glos 1982) Pumpkin weight: 444 lb 0 oz (var. Own Seed, Hants 1984)
LONG WHITE TRAILING: Another large marrow, pale-skinned and excellent for storage	M				
GREEN BUSH: A popular all-rounder — cut the fruits as courgettes or marrows	M				
EARLY GEM: Another courgette/marrow all-rounder — earlier than Green Bush	M				
CUSTARD MARROW: The Patty Pan squash — flat and scalloped-edged. Cook like courgettes	SS				
SCALLOPINI: Ball-shaped and scalloped-edged. Green-skinned — cook like courgettes	SS				
VEGETABLE MARROW: Flesh scrapes out in spaghetti-like strands after boiling	SS				
TABLE ACE: One of a number of winter squashes — suitable only for southern districts	WS				
MAMMOTH: The standard variety for growing pumpkins for the vegetable show. Orange-skinned	P				
ATLANTIC GIANT: Another giant, reputed to be larger than Mammoth or Hundredweight	P				

M Marrow variety WS Winter squash variety
SS Summer squash variety P Pumpkin variety

Calendar

Sow outdoors in late May or early June. In the Midlands and northern areas cover the seedlings with cloches if you can for a few weeks. The first squashes will be ready in July.

For an earlier crop sow seeds under glass in late April. Plant out the seedlings in early June when the danger of frost has passed.

	JAN	FEB	MAR	APR	MAY	JUN	JUL	AUG	SEP	OCT	NOV	DEC
Recommended Sowing Time (outdoors)					■							
Actual Sowing Dates (outdoors)												
Recommended Sowing Time (under glass)				■		■						
Actual Sowing Dates (under glass)												
Expected Cutting Time								■	■	■		
Actual Cutting Dates												

For key to symbols — see page 7

page 37

ONION & SHALLOT from sets

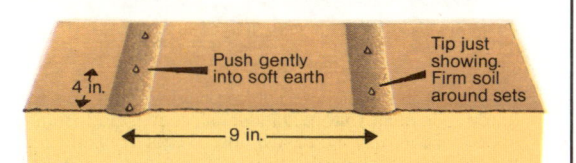

An onion set is an immature bulb which has been specially grown for planting. There are many advantages in choosing sets rather than seed. Mildew and onion fly do not attack, high soil fertility and good growing conditions are not necessary and less work is involved. An impressive list, but there are two drawbacks. Sets are a more expensive way of growing onions and there is an extra risk of running to seed (bolting). Bolting is now less of a problem than it used to be as modern varieties are more resistant than the older ones. As a further safeguard buy sets which have been heat-treated and are no larger than ¾ in. across. Shallots are milder in flavour than onions and the ones you buy are already full-sized — they quickly start to grow after planting and produce in summer a cluster of 8–12 similar-sized bulbs.

Push gently into soft earth — *Tip just showing. Firm soil around sets* — 4 in. — 9 in.

Onion sets are planted 4 in. apart — shallots require wider (6 in.) spacing. If planting has to be delayed, open the package and spread out the sets in a cool, well-lit place to prevent premature sprouting.

Protect the sets from birds if they are a nuisance in your area. Use netting rather than black thread. Keep the bed weed-free by hoeing or hand pulling. Push back any sets which have been lifted by frost or birds.

Treat as for seed-sown onions once the onion sets are established and shoots have appeared (see page 38).

Harvesting

Shallots are harvested in July when the leaves turn yellow. Lift and separate the clusters. Remove dirt and dead stems and allow the bulbs to dry. Store in nets or nylon tights in a cool dry place — the bulbs should last for about 8 months.
See page 38 for onion harvesting details.

Varieties

Variety	Type	Variety grown	Yield, flavour & notes for next year	Expected yield
STUTTGARTER GIANT: Flat, mild-flavoured onions with good keeping qualities. An old favourite	O			7 lb from a 10 ft row
STURON: A modern variety — large, round bulbs with excellent bolt resistance	O			
AILSA CRAIG: An old favourite — round and large with white, mild-flavoured flesh	O			
GIANT FEN GLOBE: A large, pale yellow and round onion. Sometimes listed as Rijnsburger	O			
MARSHALLS SHOWMASTER: A new variety — heat-treated and capable of producing 2 lb onions	O			
DUTCH YELLOW: The basic shallot variety — offered under various names — e.g Giant Yellow	S			
LONGKEEPING YELLOW: A modern shallot, chosen for its outstanding storage qualities	S			
SANTE: An exhibition and kitchen variety — bulbs are large and round	S			
HATIVE DE NIORT: The usual choice by exhibitors — perfectly shaped with deep brown skins	S			

O Onion variety
S Shallot variety

Calendar

	JAN	FEB	MAR	APR	MAY	JUN	JUL	AUG	SEP	OCT	NOV	DEC
Recommended Sowing Time		■	■	■								
Actual Sowing Dates												
Expected Lifting Time							■	■	■			
Actual Lifting Dates												

Onion sets are planted between mid March and mid April. Shallots are planted earlier — from mid February to mid March.

For key to symbols — see page 7

VEGETABLES A–Z

ONION from seed

Nowadays it is possible to obtain onions fresh from the garden or out of store almost all year round from a couple of carefully-timed sowings. It is not a difficult crop to care for — the secret lies in careful preparation before sowing. Choose a well-drained and sunny site — dig in autumn, incorporate compost and lime if necessary. Before sowing prepare a traditional 'onion bed'. Apply Growmore and rake over the surface when the soil is reasonably dry. Tread over the area and then rake again to produce a fine, even tilth.

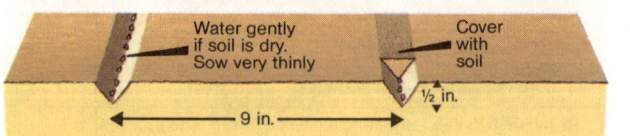

Thin the spring-sown crop in 2 stages — first to 1–2 in. apart when the seedlings have straightened up and then to 4 in. at the small 'spring onion' stage. Lift carefully — remove thinnings which attract onion fly. Seeds of Japanese varieties should be sown 1 in. apart – thin to 4 in. spacings. Salad onion rows should be 4 in. apart.

Seedlings raised under glass should be planted 4 in. apart. Roots must fall vertically in the hole — bulb base should be ½ in. below the surface.

Hoe carefully or weed by hand. Water if the weather is dry and occasionally feed with a liquid fertilizer. Mulching cuts down the need for weeding and watering. Stop watering once the bulbs have swollen. Pull back the earth or mulch to expose the bulb surface to the sun. Break off any flower stalks which appear.

Harvesting

Pull the Salad varieties when the bulbs are ½–1 in. across — the season is between March and October. With Bulb varieties wait for about 2 weeks after the foliage has turned yellow and toppled over. Lift with a fork on a dry day. Standard Bulb onions which are not for immediate use should be dried and stored. Spread out on sacking or in trays — outdoors if it is sunny and indoors if the weather is rainy. Drying will take 7–21 days. Inspect carefully — use damaged and thick-necked ones immediately. Store sound ones in trays, net bags or nylon tights — or you can tie to a length of cord. Keep in a cool and well-lit place.

Types

STANDARD BULB varieties & JAPANESE BULB varieties

The Standard varieties are grown for their large bulbs which can be stored throughout the winter months. Some have a flattened shape, others are globular. Skin colours vary from almost pure white to bright red and flavours range from mild to strong. Most of them are only suitable for spring sowing but some can be sown in August for a late July crop. The Japanese varieties make late summer sowing a much more reliable routine but their midsummer crop cannot be stored.

SALAD varieties

Thinnings of the Bulb varieties can be used as salad or 'spring' onions, but there are several varieties which are grown specifically for salad use. These Salad varieties, also known as scallions or bunching onions, are white-skinned and mild-flavoured.

PICKLING varieties

Several onion varieties are grown for their small silverskin bulbs (button onions) which are lifted in July or August and pickled for use as cocktail onions. These varieties should be sown in April in sandy soil — do not feed. The seedlings should not be thinned.

Calendar

For an August or September crop sow as soon as the land is workable in the spring (late February–early April depending on the location of your garden).

Sow in mid August for an earlier crop. Japanese varieties mature in late June — Standard varieties such as Reliance and Ailsa Craig are less hardy, less reliable and later cropping (late July onwards), but they can be stored.

In cold areas and for exhibition bulbs sow under glass in January, harden off in March and transplant outdoors in April.

Salad onions should be sown in March–July for a June–October crop. Sow in August for onions in March–May.

	JAN	FEB	MAR	APR	MAY	JUN	JUL	AUG	SEP	OCT	NOV	DEC
Recommended Sowing Time (outdoors)			■	■				■				
Actual Sowing Dates (outdoors)												
Recommended Sowing Time (under glass)	■			✿								
Actual Sowing Dates (under glass)												
Expected Lifting Time							■	■	■			
Actual Lifting Dates												

For key to symbols — see page 7

Varieties

Name	Type	Shape
AILSA CRAIG: The one that is in all the catalogues. Very large and a show winner. Recommended for sowing under glass in January	SB	
BEDFORDSHIRE CHAMPION: Like Ailsa Craig it is large, globular and popular. It keeps much better, but it is more susceptible to mildew	SB	
RIJNSBURGER: Large and white-fleshed — the strain Balstora is a late variety with outstanding storage qualities. Onions last until May	SB	
HYGRO: An F_1 hybrid of Rijnsburger — uniform and long-keeping like its parent. Heavy, mild-flavoured and pale-skinned	SB	
BUFFALO: A new F_1 hybrid which produces an early crop. Thin-necked and very hard but not suitable for storage	SB	
LANCASTRIAN: Described as the 'giant onion' in the catalogues — a good choice for exhibition and also for kitchen use. Stores well	SB	
RELIANCE: Perhaps the best of the Standard varieties for sowing in August. The bulbs are large and the keeping qualities are outstanding	SB	
JAMES LONG KEEPING: An old favourite with reddish-brown skins. Good flavour and excellent keeping qualities. Unfortunately it is hard to find	SB	
CARMEN: A fairly standard globular onion, but the shiny red skin makes it different. The old reds have gone from the catalogues	SB	
EXPRESS YELLOW: The earliest of the Japanese varieties, but the yields are not outstanding. Flattish bulbs with yellow skins	JB	
KAIZUKA EXTRA EARLY: Like Express Yellow the skin is yellow but (despite the name) it matures a little later. Flattish, like most Japanese varieties	JB	
IMAI EARLY YELLOW: A yellow globular or semi-globular onion which is ready for pulling in late June, a little later than Express Yellow	JB	
SENSHYU: A Japanese variety which is rather similar to Imai Early Yellow, but the bulbs are flatter and it matures about 2 weeks later	JB	
WHITE LISBON: By far the most popular of the Salad varieties. Quick-growing and silvery-skinned — provides spring onions for 6 months	S	
WINTER WHITE BUNCHING: Sow in August or September for pulling in May. Slow to form bulbs but this variety is very hardy	S	
ISHIKURA: A distinctive type of Salad onion — the long stems do not form bulbs — pull out alternate plants and leave remainder to mature	S	
PARIS SILVERSKIN: The most popular Pickling variety. No need to thin — pull when the bulb is the size of a marble	P	
BARLETTA: Offered by a few nurserymen as an alternative to Paris Silverskin — no particular advantages or disadvantages between the two	P	

Expected yield: 8 lb from a 10 ft row

U.K. record: Weight: 9 lb 1 oz (var. *Unknown*, Lancs 1988)

SB Standard bulb variety
JB Japanese bulb variety
S Salad variety
P Pickling variety

VEGETABLES A-Z

PARSNIP

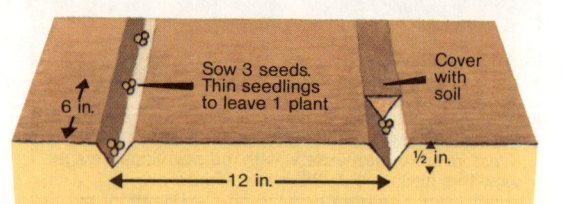

Before the potato came to Britain from the New World, it was the parsnip which accompanied meat, game and fish. Nowadays it is regarded as too sweet and too strongly-flavoured to be a potato substitute, and so its popularity is low. This is a pity, as it is an easy crop to grow and there are recipes which can turn this vegetable Cinderella into a tasty dish. Any reasonable soil will do for its cultivation, but you will need deep, friable and stone-free soil if you want to grow long and tapering roots.

Sow 3 seeds. Thin seedlings to leave 1 plant. Cover with soil. 6 in. / 12 in. / ½ in.

Seed is very light — sow on a still day. Germination is slow in cold weather. Parsnips seldom produce satisfactory roots after transplanting — throw thinnings away.

Hoe regularly to keep down weeds — do not touch the crowns of the plants. Very few pests attack parsnips — squash between the fingers the leaf blisters containing celery fly grubs.

Watering is required only when there is a prolonged dry spell.

Harvesting

The roots are ready for cropping when the foliage starts to die in autumn. Lift as required, using a fork to loosen the soil. This lifting can continue throughout the winter, but it is a good idea to harvest and store some in November to overcome the frozen soil problem in mid winter. Lift all remaining roots in late February.

Varieties

Variety	Type	Variety grown	Yield, flavour & notes for next year	Expected yield	U.K. record
TENDER AND TRUE: The most popular long variety — little core plus good canker resistance	L			8 lb from a 10 ft row	Weight: 10 lb 9 oz (var. *Tender and True*, E. Sussex 1980) Length: 143 in. (var. *Tender and True*, Dyfed 1984)
HOLLOW CROWN IMPROVED: Another long one for kitchen and exhibition use. Yields are high	L				
EXHIBITION: Lives up to its name — roots are extra-long for showing	L				
LISBONNAIS: A heavy cropping variety with smooth skins and fine texture	L				
GLADIATOR: The first F$_1$ hybrid parsnip. Matures very early — good canker resistance	L				
OFFENHAM: For years the most popular medium-sized parsnip, but not recommended these days	M				
WHITE GEM: Canker resistant — has taken over from the similar Offenham. Good flavour	M				
THE STUDENT: Thick and tapering — the one to choose for top flavour	M				
COBHAM IMPROVED MARROW: Tapering smooth-skinned roots. Good resistance to canker	M				
AVONRESISTER: The one for poor soils — 5 in. cones which are canker resistant	S				

L Long variety
M Medium-length variety
S Short variety

Calendar

Use fresh seed every year. February is the traditional month for sowing parsnips, but it is better to wait until March. Sow short-rooted varieties in April.

	JAN	FEB	MAR	APR	MAY	JUN	JUL	AUG	SEP	OCT	NOV	DEC
Recommended Sowing Time												
Actual Sowing Dates												
Expected Lifting Time												
Actual Lifting Dates												

For key to symbols — see page 7

PEA

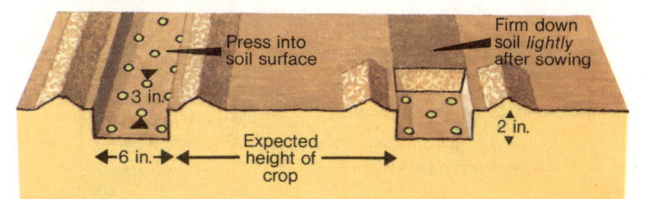

If you want to taste just how good peas can be then pick the pods when the peas inside are still quite small. Within an hour boil the shelled peas for about 10 minutes in a small amount of water. Delicious, but peas are often disappointing as a garden crop. Yields can be quite small, and if the soil is poor and the weather is hot then the amount obtained may not be worth the trouble taken. The secret of obtaining a worthwhile crop is to follow the basic rules. Choose the right variety for the sowing date, make sure the soil is fertile, never sow in cold and wet soil, keep the birds away, spray when necessary, provide support as required and pick the pods at regular intervals.

Treat the seed with a fungicidal dressing if it is to be sown in early spring. Immediately after sowing you must protect the rows from birds. Several methods are used — black cotton stretched between short stakes, plastic netting, twiggy branches over the drills etc, but best of all are wire-mesh guards. Make sure the ends are closed.

Hoe regularly to keep weeds under control. When the seedlings are about 3 in. high insert twigs alongside the stems to provide support. You must not delay this task — leaving the stems laying on the ground will result in severe slug damage if the weather is wet. Medium- and tall-growing varieties need extra support — erect a screen of plastic netting along each row.

Water during dry spells in summer. Apply a mulch between the rows in order to conserve moisture. Pea moth is often a problem — to prevent maggoty peas spray the plants with fenitrothion 7–10 days after the start of flowering.

Harvesting

Start harvesting when the pods are well filled but there is still a little space between each pea. Begin at the bottom of the stem and work upwards — use two hands, one to hold the stem and the other to pick off the pod. Pick regularly — pods left to mature on the plant will hasten the end of flowering and fruiting. If you harvest too many to cook immediately, place the excess in the refrigerator or deep-freeze. Pick mangetout when the pods are about 3 in. long and the peas within are just starting to develop. Asparagus peas are ready when they are 1–1½ in. long. After harvest use the stems of all pea varieties for making compost, but leave the roots in the ground.

Types

ROUND varieties
The seeds of these varieties remain smooth and round when dried. They are all First Earlies — hardier and quicker-maturing than other types and more able to withstand poor growing conditions than the Wrinkled types. Round varieties are used for late autumn and early spring sowing.

WRINKLED varieties
The seeds of these varieties are distinctly wrinkled when dried. These 'marrowfat' peas are sweeter, larger and heavier cropping than the Round ones, and are therefore much more widely grown. They are, however, less hardy and should not be sown before March. These Wrinkled varieties are classified in two ways. Firstly by height (there are the 1½–2 ft dwarfs and the 4–5 ft tall varieties) and secondly by the time taken from sowing to first picking. First Earlies take 11–12 weeks, Second Earlies 13–14 weeks and Maincrop 15–16 weeks. In catalogues and garden centres you will find a large choice from each group.

MANGETOUT varieties
There are several names for this group — chinese peas, snow peas, sugar peas and eat-all. They are rather easier to grow than garden peas — pick before the seeds swell and cook the pods whole.

PETIT POIS varieties
Petit pois are not immature peas gathered from small pods of any garden pea variety — they are a small number of dwarf varieties which produce tiny (⅛–¼ in.) peas which are uniquely sweet.

ASPARAGUS PEA variety
This variety is also known as the winged pea. It is not really a pea at all — it is a vetch which produces sprawling bushy plants. It is not frost-hardy, so sowing must be delayed until May. The red flowers which appear in summer are followed by curiously shaped winged pods — these must be gathered whilst they are still small or they will be fibrous and stringy. The small pods are cooked whole like mangetout.

PEA continued

Calendar

		JAN	FEB	MAR	APR	MAY	JUN	JUL	AUG	SEP	OCT	NOV	DEC
For a May/June Crop Choose a sheltered site — expect some losses if the site is cold and exposed. Grow a Round variety — Feltham First is reliable for both early spring and late sowing. Meteor has an excellent reputation for hardiness. Cover seedlings and plants with cloches.	Recommended Sowing Time		■	■							■	■	
	Actual Sowing Dates												
	Expected Picking Time						■						
	Actual Picking Dates												
For a June/July Crop For a mid March sowing choose a Round variety or a First Early Wrinkled variety such as Kelvedon Wonder, Hurst Beagle or Early Onward. For late March or April sowing pick a Second Early Wrinkled type — Onward is the usual choice but Hurst Green Shaft is a good alternative.	Recommended Sowing Time				■								
	Actual Sowing Dates												
	Expected Picking Time							■					
	Actual Picking Dates												
For an August Crop Use a Maincrop Wrinkled variety — be guided by the height on the back of the packet rather than the pretty picture on the front. If space is limited choose a medium-height pea such as Senator — leave Alderman for the people who can spare 5 ft between the rows.	Recommended Sowing Time					■							
	Actual Sowing Dates												
	Expected Picking Time								■	■			
	Actual Picking Dates												
For an Autumn Crop Fresh peas are especially welcome in September and October when the main picking season is over. June–July is the sowing season and you must choose the right type — a First Early Wrinkled variety with good mildew resistance. Kelvedon Wonder will not let you down.	Recommended Sowing Time							■					
	Actual Sowing Dates												
	Expected Picking Time									■	■		
	Actual Picking Dates												
Mangetout & Petit pois Sow seed when the soil has started to warm up in April — sowing can be delayed until May. Neither mangetout nor petit pois have become popular like the familiar garden peas — you may have to send off for seeds if your local garden shop does not carry them.	Recommended Sowing Time			■	■	■							
	Actual Sowing Dates												
	Expected Picking Time								■	■			
	Actual Picking Dates												
Asparagus Pea Sow seed in mid or late May so that the seedlings will appear after the last frosts have gone. Make 1 in. deep drills about 15 in. apart and sow seeds at 6 in. intervals. The harvest period usually starts at the beginning of August and continues for many weeks.	Recommended Sowing Time					■							
	Actual Sowing Dates												
	Expected Picking Time								■	■			
	Actual Picking Dates												

For key to symbols — see page 7

page 43

Varieties

Variety	Type	Earliness	Variety grown	Yield, flavour & notes for next year	Expected yield	U.K. record
FELTHAM FIRST: 1½ ft. You will find this old favourite in all the catalogues. Needs little support — ready 11 weeks after sowing	R	1st E				
METEOR: 1 ft. The baby of the group. Very hardy — recommended for cold and exposed sites. This is the one for February sowing	R	1st E				
DOUCE PROVENCE: 1½ ft. This is the one to choose if you want the hardiness and earliness of a Round variety coupled with sweetness	R	1st E				
KELVEDON WONDER: 1½ ft. A popular variety with good mildew resistance. Suitable for both early spring and summer sowing. Pods narrow and pointed	W	1st E				
EARLY ONWARD: 2 ft. Its famous big brother (Onward) is a Second Early — this one is similar but matures about 10 days earlier	W	1st E				
LITTLE MARVEL: 1½ ft. Listed in most catalogues — a heavy cropper with blunt-ended pods borne in pairs. Useful for early sowing	W	1st E				
HURST BEAGLE: 1½ ft. Pods are blunt and well-filled — this variety is the earliest Wrinkled variety. Good reputation for sweetness	W	1st E				
GRADUS: 4 ft. A tall variety amongst the First Early dwarfs. Pods are dark green, pointed and plentiful. Matures very early	W	1st E				
ONWARD: 2½ ft. The most popular garden pea — crops heavily and has good disease resistance. Sometimes classed as an Early Maincrop	W	2nd E			10 lb from a 10 ft row	Length: 10⅝ in. (var. *Show Perfection*, Roxburgh 1964)
HURST GREEN SHAFT: 2½ ft. Another popular Second Early — the pointed pods are borne at the top of the plant. Resistant to mildew	W	2nd E				
LINCOLN: 1½ ft. The pods are small but yields are abundant and the peas are very sweet. Appears in only a few catalogues	W	2nd E				
ALDERMAN: 5 ft. The giant amongst the Maincrops — height, yields and pod length are all large. The picking season lasts a long time	W	M				
SENATOR: 2½ ft. The Maincrop for the smaller garden. The pods are borne in pairs and are noted for their abundance and sweetness	W	M				
OREGON SUGAR POD: 3½ ft. A popular variety listed in many catalogues. The fleshy, curved pods can reach 4–4½ in. but pick at the 3 in. stage	MT	—				
SUGAR DWARF SWEET GREEN: 3 ft. Similar to Oregon Sugar Pod — catalogues tend to list one or the other and there is little to choose between them	MT	—				
SUGAR SNAP: 5 ft. Pods are thick and fleshy. Cook as mangetout when pods are small or leave to mature and treat like french beans	MT	—				
WAVEREX: 2 ft. The most popular petit pois variety. Yield of blunt-ended pods is high — peas are tiny and very sweet	P	—				
ASPARAGUS PEA: 1 ft. A large number of small pods appear at the end of July and cropping usually continues for about 2 months	A	—				

VEGETABLES A-Z

Round variety — R — 1st E — First Early garden pea
Wrinkled variety — W — 2nd E — Second Early garden pea
Mangetout variety — MT — M — Maincrop garden pea
Petit pois variety — P
Asparagus Pea variety — A

POTATO

One of the advantages of growing your own potatoes is that you can choose the variety to suit you from a wide range of shapes, sizes, colours and textures. The skin may be red, yellow or white — the flesh may be white, pale cream or distinctly yellow. Texture is waxy or floury and the shape round, oval or long. This vegetable can be grown in practically any soil type — it is the best crop to grow in wasteland which is to be turned into a vegetable plot. In the established plot potatoes should not be grown on land which has been used for this vegetable within the past two seasons. Dig in autumn — liming is rarely necessary. Rake in Bromophos in spring if there is a wireworm problem.

Seed potatoes should be the size of a small hen's egg (1–2 oz) — large seed should not be cut in half. Do not use soft or diseased ones. Set out seed potatoes in peat-filled wooden trays in February — eyed ends uppermost. Keep in a light, frost-free place until several sturdy ½–1 in. shoots are present.

Earth-up when the stems are about 9 in. tall. Break up the soil between the rows and use a draw hoe to pile loose earth against the stems to produce a flat-topped ridge about 6 in. high. Earth-up a little at a time or do it as a one-step operation — it makes no difference.

Water copiously in dry weather — this is very important once tubers have started to form.

Harvesting

Earlies are ready for harvesting when the tubers are hen's egg size — insert a flat-tined fork into the ridge and lift roots forward. With Maincrops for storage wait until the stems have withered. Cut the stems at near ground level and remove — after 10 days lift the tubers and leave them to dry for several hours. Place in wooden boxes and keep in a dark, frost-free place.

Types

FIRST EARLY varieties
Potatoes grown for harvesting in June or July. These early-maturing varieties do not produce high yields, but they are ready when shop prices are high. They take up less space than Maincrops and are not subject to the ravages of blight. First Earlies are not generally grown for storage — lifting takes place when the tubers are quite small and they are treated as new potatoes for immediate cooking.

SECOND EARLY varieties
A small and declining group of potato varieties which bridge the gap between the First Earlies of July and the Maincrops of autumn. Sometimes called Mid-season varieties.

MAINCROP varieties
Potatoes grown for maximum yields of tubers — these potatoes are stored for winter use. Some lists separate Early Maincrops which are ready in early or mid September (Desirée, Maris Piper etc) from Late Maincrops (Golden Wonder etc) which are harvested in late September or October.

Calendar

First Early varieties: Plant seed potatoes in late March — a week or two earlier in southerly areas and a couple of weeks later in the north. Harvest in June or July.
Second Early varieties: Plant in early–mid April and lift in July or August.
Maincrop varieties: Plant in mid–late April. Some of the tubers can be lifted in August for immediate use but potatoes for storage should be harvested in September or early October.

	JAN	FEB	MAR	APR	MAY	JUN	JUL	AUG	SEP	OCT	NOV	DEC
Recommended Planting Time			■	■								
Actual Planting Dates												
Expected Lifting Time							■	■	■	■		
Actual Lifting Dates												

For key to symbols — see page 7

page 45

Varieties

	Earliness	Shape	Variety grown	Yield, flavour & notes for next year	Expected yield	U.K. record
SUTTON'S FOREMOST: White skin and white flesh. This variety has a good reputation for high yields and for staying firm when boiled	1st E					
EPICURE: White skin and white flesh. An old variety which is hardier than most First Earlies, but it is non-immune to wart disease	1st E					
MARIS BARD: White skin and white waxy flesh. A popular First Early which is perhaps the earliest and heaviest yielder of the group	1st E					
PENTLAND JAVELIN: White skin and white waxy flesh. Matures rather late but the crop is heavy and it is scab-resistant. May blacken after cooking	1st E					
ULSTER SCEPTRE: White skin and white waxy flesh. An aggressive grower — useful when the land is weedy. Yields are good — a popular variety	1st E					
HOME GUARD: White skin and white waxy flesh. An old variety dating back to World War II. Does well in heavy soils	1st E				Early varieties: 12 lb from a 10 ft row / Maincrop varieties: 20 lb from a 10 ft row	Weight: 7 lb 1 oz (var. *Arran Pilot*, Warwicks 1982)
ESTIMA: White skin and pale yellow waxy flesh. Crops heavily and is a good chip variety. A popular choice suitable for exhibiting	2nd E					
WILJA: White skin and pale yellow waxy flesh. Another popular Dutch Second Early. Liable to blacken after cooking	2nd E					
MARIS PEER: White skin and white waxy flesh. Some resistance to scab and blight, but fails miserably in dry soil	2nd E					
BAILLIE: White skin and white flesh. The successor to the old favourite Great Scot. Good blight resistance — can be stored for winter use	2nd E					
MARIS PIPER: White skin and pale creamy floury flesh. A popular successor to Majestic but scab, slug and drought resistance are low	M					
DESIREE: Pink skin and pale creamy flesh. A good choice — heavy crops, good drought resistance and robust growth, but susceptible to scab	M					
PENTLAND CROWN: White skin and white waxy flesh. Good disease resistance and very heavy yields, but its cooking qualities are only moderate	M					
PENTLAND SQUIRE: White skin and white flesh. High yielding like Pentland Crown, but it is earlier and the cooking properties are better	M					
PENTLAND DELL: White skin and white flesh. An Early Maincrop which is suitable for exhibiting. Not very good for boiling but excellent for baking	M					
KING EDWARD: Red-blotched skin and creamy flesh. Good for baking. Not a heavy cropper and not immune to wart disease	M					
GOLDEN WONDER: Russet skin and yellow floury flesh. Renowned for flavour but needs good soil and good growing conditions to give a satisfactory crop	M					
PINK FIR APPLE: Pink skin and yellow flesh. The long irregular tubers have a new-potato flavour — good for potato salad. Disappointing yields	M					

1st E *First Early variety*
2nd E *Second Early variety*
M *Maincrop variety*

VEGETABLES A-Z

RADISH

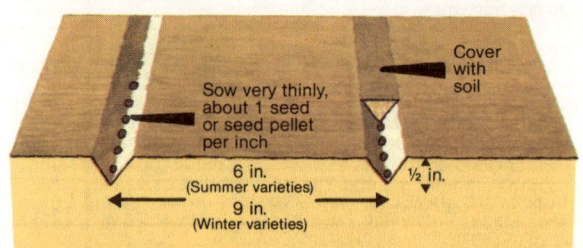

The popular ones are the Summer varieties which garnish the salad plate. Most (but not all) are small and the usual colour is red or a red/white mixture. There are variations — the Japanese types can grow 1 ft long and there are all-white varieties. The Winter varieties are not popular and only a few are listed in the catalogues. These have white, black or pink skins and may weigh up to several pounds. The flavour is stronger than the Summer types.

Sow very thinly, about 1 seed or seed pellet per inch. Cover with soil. 6 in. (Summer varieties) / 9 in. (Winter varieties) / ½ in.

With the Summer varieties little or no thinning is required — if necessary thin to 1 in. (small radishes) or 2–4 in. (larger and Japanese radishes). Thin Winter varieties to 6 in. apart. Protect against birds if they are a nuisance in your area. Spray with derris if flea beetles appear.

Hoe and water as necessary. Regular watering in dry weather is essential if woody and peppery roots are to be avoided.

Harvesting

Pull globular Summer varieties when they are 5p sized and medium-length ones when they are no longer than your thumb. Pull the Japanese types when they are 6 in. long. Leave Winter varieties in the ground and pull as required — cover the crowns with peat. Alternatively lift in November and store.

Varieties

Variety	Type	Expected yield	U.K. record
CHERRY BELLE: Cherry-coloured on the outside — white, crisp and mild inside	S		
SCARLET GLOBE: A quick-maturing variety — useful for early spring sowing	S		
PRINZ RUTIN: Also known as Red Prince. Remains non-woody even when large	S	Summer varieties: 4 lb from a 10 ft row	
SAXERRE: The variety to choose for sowing under cloches in January/February	S		Weight: 17 lb 0 oz (var. Minowase Summer, Powys 1976)
SPARKLER: Bright scarlet, distinctively tipped with white. Quick growing and mild	S		
FRENCH BREAKFAST: The popular medium-length type — mild when harvested early	S		
LONG WHITE ICICLE: An excellent choice — 3 in. long radishes which are crisp and nutty-flavoured	S	Winter varieties: 10 lb from a 10 ft row	
MINOWASE SUMMER: A Japanese type — can grow 12 in. long but harvest at 6 in. stage	S		
APRIL CROSS: Another Japanese or mooli type — can be sown in spring. Reaches 12 in. long	S		
CHINA ROSE: Large oval roots up to 1 lb in weight. Flesh white and crisp	W		
BLACK SPANISH ROUND: Large, black-skinned and round. Flesh is white	W		

S Summer variety
W Winter variety

Calendar

Summer varieties: Sow under cloches in January or February or outdoors in March. For a prolonged supply sow every few weeks or try 'Mixed Radish' seed which contains varieties which mature at different times. Sowing after early June often gives disappointing results.

Winter varieties: Sow in July or early August. Lift roots from late October onwards.

For key to symbols — see page 7

SPINACH

There are two types of true spinach and both are annuals. The Summer varieties have round seeds and grow quickly under good conditions to produce a tender crop throughout the summer months. The Winter varieties usually have prickly seeds and provide a useful crop of greens from October to April. The New Zealand variety is not a true spinach — it is a dwarf and rambling plant which produces mild-flavoured leaves.

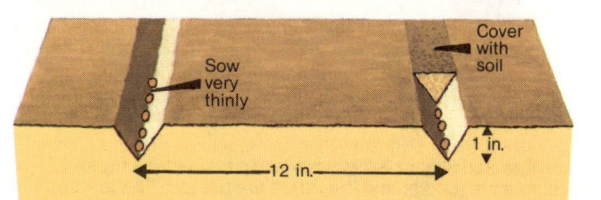

Sow very thinly — 12 in. — *Cover with soil, 1 in.*

New Zealand spinach needs more space than shown above. Sow 3 seeds in a group ¾ in. deep. Leave 2 ft between the groups. Thin each group to 1 plant when the seedlings are large enough to handle.

Thin Summer and Winter varieties to 3 in. apart as soon as they are large enough to handle. Two weeks later remove alternate plants.

Hoe as necessary — water copiously in dry weather. Cover Winter varieties with cloches or straw from October onwards.

Harvesting

Start picking as soon as the leaves are a reasonable size — pick only young and tender leaves. Pick continually. With Summer varieties you can remove up to half the foliage — with Winter varieties pick much more sparingly. Remove just a few basal leaves of New Zealand spinach at each picking session.

Varieties

	Type	Variety grown	Yield, flavour & notes for next year	Expected yield
KING OF DENMARK: An old favourite. Resistance to bolting is not good — choose a modern variety	S			
BLOOMSDALE: A deep green variety with reasonable resistance to bolting	S			
SIGMALEAF: Can be sown in autumn as a Winter variety. Slow to bolt	S			5-10 lb from a 10 ft row
NORVAK: High yielding and slow to bolt even in midsummer	S			
VIKING: Another modern Summer variety which is slow to run to seed	S			
MELODY: An F$_1$ hybrid with dark leaves which tolerate mosaic virus	S			
SYMPHONY: Another F$_1$ hybrid which like Melody has dark green leaves. Erect growth habit	S			
MEDANIA: A modern variety which produces an abundant supply of leaves	S			
BROAD-LEAVED PRICKLY: Foliage is dark and fleshy, and the plants are slow to bolt	W			
MONNOPA: A fine-flavoured variety which has a low oxalic acid content	W			
NEW ZEALAND SPINACH: Listed in most catalogues — flourishes in dry weather without bolting	NZ			

S Summer variety
W Winter variety
NZ New Zealand variety

Calendar

Summer varieties: Sow every few weeks from mid March to the end of May for picking between late May and the end of October.

Winter varieties: Sow in August and again in September for picking between October and April.

New Zealand variety: Sow in late May for picking between June and September.

	JAN	FEB	MAR	APR	MAY	JUN	JUL	AUG	SEP	OCT	NOV	DEC
Recommended Sowing Time			■	■	■			■	■			
Actual Sowing Dates												
Expected Picking Time	■	■	■	■		■	■	■	■	■	■	■
Actual Picking Dates												

For key to symbols — see page 7

VEGETABLES A-Z

SWEDE

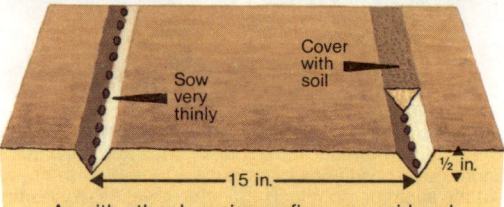

Swedes are closely related to turnips but the flesh is generally yellow and flavour is both milder and sweeter. In addition the plants are hardier and the yields are greater. The introduction of disease-resistant varieties has made this winter vegetable even easier to grow. All you have to do is sprinkle some seed in late spring or early summer, thin a few weeks later and then lift the large globular roots as you need them from autumn until spring.

Harvesting

Begin lifting as soon as the roots are large enough to use. This will be from early autumn onwards — you can leave them in the soil until required. However, frozen soil in winter can be a problem so it may be more convenient to lift and store indoors in December. To store, twist off leaves and place roots between layers of peat in a box. Store in a cool place.

As with other brassicas a firm, non-acid and reasonably free-draining soil is required. Apply Bromophos before sowing if cabbage root fly is known to be a problem.

Thin out as soon as the seedlings are large enough to handle. Do this in stages until the plants are 9 in. apart.

Hoe as necessary. Water copiously in dry weather — failure to do so will result in woody roots. Rain following a dry spell will cause the roots to split if the soil has not been watered.

Spray with derris or Crop Saver at the first signs of flea beetle damage.

Varieties

Variety	Description	Expected yield
MARIAN:	Purple-topped variety — the one to choose. Excellent disease resistance	
WESTERN PERFECTION:	An almost neckless variety. Early — may be ready for lifting in September	
MANCUNIAN BROWN TOP:	The opposite to Western Perfection — slow growing but stores well	
PURPLE TOP:	An old favourite — reliable and suitable for eating fresh or keeping in store	30 lb from a 10 ft row
BEST OF ALL:	A medium-sized swede which is very hardy and stores well. Mild flavour	
ACME:	A quick-growing variety like Western Perfection. The flesh is orange	
WILHELMSBURGER GELBE:	Another early variety. It is pink-topped and the flesh is almost fibre-free	
CHIGNECTO:	A club root-resistant variety. In the text-books but not in the catalogues	
MAGNIFICENT:	A large-rooted variety with a good reputation for hardiness. Firm flesh	

Calendar

In order to avoid mildew it is usual to delay sowing swedes until May or early June. In dry weather water the drills before sowing.

Recommended Sowing Time: May–June
Expected Lifting Time: Jan–Mar, Sep–Dec

For key to symbols — see page 7

SWEET CORN

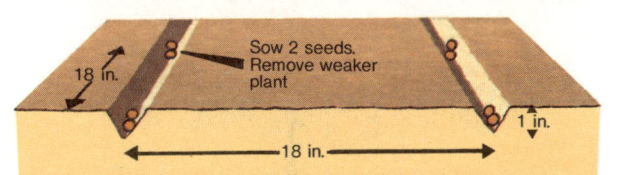

There is still a widespread view that sweet corn cannot be grown outside the southern counties, but this is no longer true. Choose one of the F_1 hybrids which have revolutionised the reliability of sweet corn in this country — the Older ('open-pollinating') varieties produce heavy crops but require a better climate than ours. Grow sweet corn in a sheltered sunny spot and the plants should not disappoint you even as far north as Lancashire or Yorkshire.

Sow or plant in rectangular blocks, not in rows. This will ensure effective wind pollination of the female flowers. When raising plants under glass sow 2 seeds in 3 in. pots and take out the weaker seedling.

Remove cloches when the foliage touches the glass. Protect from birds — hoe around plants as necessary. Cover surface roots with soil — do not remove side shoots.

Water in dry weather. Stake tall plants and in summer tap the tassels at the top of each stem to aid pollination.

Harvesting

Test for ripeness when the silks on top of the cob have turned dark brown. Pull back part of the sheath and squeeze a couple of grains — the liquid which oozes out should be creamy but not watery. Carefully twist the ripe cob off the stem. Do this just before it is required for cooking.

Varieties

Variety	Type	Variety grown	Yield, flavour & notes for next year	Expected yield
EARLY XTRA SWEET: A little later than the early ones, but very sweet	F_1			1–2 cobs per plant
FIRST OF ALL: One of the earliest — a good variety for the midlands and northern areas	F_1			
EARLIKING: Medium height with large cobs. An early variety noted for reliability	F_1			
KELVEDON SWEETHEART: Medium height — claimed to be an improvement on Earliking	F_1			
JOHN INNES HYBRID: A popular choice — early, reliable and vigorous with medium-sized cobs	F_1			
NORTH STAR: Large cobs. The choice of many experts for northern districts	F_1			
AZTEC: An early variety noted for its long cobs with tightly-packed kernels	F_1			
SUNDANCE: Another large-cobbed variety — a good choice in poor summers	F_1			
KELVEDON GLORY: A popular mid-season variety. Cobs are large and well-filled	F_1			
GOLDEN BANTAM: The only Older variety you are likely to find	O			

F_1 F_1 hybrid variety
O Older variety

Calendar

Southern counties: Sow outdoors in mid May — the cobs should be ready for picking in late August or September. For extra reliability and an earlier crop (late July onwards in mild areas) sow under glass as described below.

Other counties: Sow seeds under glass in mid April–early May and plant out in late May–early June. Alternatively sow outdoors under cloches in mid May — place cloches in position about 2 weeks before sowing.

For key to symbols — see page 7

TOMATO, GREENHOUSE

Tomatoes are the main greenhouse crop in this country. It is of course extremely satisfying to pick succulent fruit from June to October, but there is a lot of work involved for the reward obtained. The plants need constant care — in summer it is necessary to water growing bags or pots at daily intervals. A wide range of pests and diseases find the tomato an ideal host and so spraying is often necessary. Still, the fascination is there and the beginner should carefully read what to do. Greenhouse varieties are cordon (single-stemmed) varieties which reach 6 ft or more if not stopped. They can be grown in border soil but it is much better to use 9 in. pots or growing bags.

Sow a couple of seeds in each 3 in. pot of compost, removing the weaker seedling after germination. Alternatively buy plants from a reputable supplier.

Plant out into growing bags, pots or border soil when the seedlings are 6–8 in. high and the flowers of the first truss are beginning to open. In border soil plant 18 in. apart.

Tie the main stem to a cane or vertical string. Cut or pinch out side shoots when they are 1 in. long. When the plants are 4 ft tall remove the leaves below the first truss. Remove yellowing leaves as the season progresses, but never overdo deleafing.

Water and feed regularly — mist plants and tap supports occasionally. Ventilate and shade in summer. When 7 trusses have set, remove tip at 2 leaves above the top truss.

Harvesting

Pick fruit when they are ripe and fully coloured. Hold the tomato in your palm and with your thumb break off the fruit at the swelling on the flower stalk. At the end of the season pick all the unripe fruit and place them as a layer in a tray. Put a couple of ripe apples next to them to generate the ripening gas ethylene. Place the tray and apples in a drawer.

Types

ORDINARY varieties
This group of red salad tomatoes contains several old favourites which are grown for reliability (Moneymaker), flavour (Ailsa Craig) or earliness (Harbinger).

F$_1$ HYBRID varieties
This group bears fruit which is similar in appearance to the Ordinary varieties, but these modern crosses have two important advantages — they are generally heavier yielding and also have a high degree of disease resistance.

BEEFSTEAK varieties
This group produces the large and meaty tomatoes which are so popular in the U.S. and on the Continent. They are excellent for sandwiches but only you can decide whether their flavour is superior to our familiar salad varieties. There are three types — the true 'beefsteak' hybrids such as Dombello, the giant hybrids such as Big Boy, and the non-hybrid Marmandes (page 53), which are suitable only for outdoor growing. Stop the plants when the fourth truss has set and provide support for the fruit if necessary.

NOVELTY varieties
Catalogues sing the praises of the yellow and striped varieties but they remain distinctly unpopular. The first tomatoes sent to Europe were gold-coloured and not red, but that was a long time ago.

Calendar

In a heated greenhouse kept at a minimum night temperature of 50°–55°F, tomato seed is sown in late December and planted out in late February or early March for a May–June crop.

Most gardeners, however, grow tomatoes in an unheated ('cold') house. Sow seed in early March and plant out in late April or early May. The first fruit will be ready for picking in July.

	JAN	FEB	MAR	APR	MAY	JUN	JUL	AUG	SEP	OCT	NOV	DEC
Recommended Sowing Time (heated greenhouse)	▮	🏠	🏠									▮
Actual Sowing Dates (heated greenhouse)												
Recommended Sowing Time (cold greenhouse)			▮ ▮	🏠 🏠								
Actual Sowing Dates (cold greenhouse)												
Expected Picking Time							░	▓	▓	░		
Actual Picking Dates												

For key to symbols — see page 7

Varieties

Variety	Type	Variety grown	Yield, flavour & notes for next year	Expected yield	U.K. record
MONEYMAKER: Still popular, but newer varieties are taking over. Trusses are large but the flavour is bland. Fruits are medium-sized	O			8 lb per plant	Weight: 5 lb 9½ oz (var. *Own Strain*, Yorks 1987)
ALICANTE: Moneymaker type — heavy cropping and reliable. There are advantages — resistant to greenback and the flavour is good	O				
AILSA CRAIG: The best-flavoured variety in the Ordinary group. Fruits are medium-sized and brightly coloured. Listed in most catalogues.	O				
HARBINGER: The earliest of the Ordinary varieties listed here. There are no other outstanding virtues, but flavour is good	O				
MONEYCROSS: A strain of Moneymaker — resistant to leaf mould and earlier than the basic species, but it is much less popular	O				
EUROCROSS: A popular choice for a heated greenhouse — large fruits on leaf mould-resistant and greenback-immune plants. Good flavour	F₁				
SHIRLEY: Few varieties can rival this one. Heavy yields, early crops, good disease resistance and unaffected by short cold spells	F₁				
HERALD: A vigorous and early-cropping variety. Tops for sweetness and flavour, according to some experts. Fruits are medium-sized	F₁				
CURABEL: The variety from which Shirley was selected — usually sold by suppliers who don't stock Shirley. Both are quite similar	F₁				
ESTRELLA: Disease resistance is the most outstanding property of this variety. Early cropping — popular with commercial growers. Fruits are large	F₁				
MINIBEL: The dwarf of the group — it can be grown in a 6 in. pot on the windowsill. No stopping is required	F₁				
IOA: An early and heavy-cropping variety which is recommended for cold houses. Disease resistance is good — fruits are medium-sized	F₁				
BIG BOY: The most popular of the giant tomatoes — fruits weigh 1 lb or more. For maximum size disbud to 3 fruits per truss	B				
DOMBELLO: A super-giant, according to the suppliers. Central core is absent and the flavour is good. Recommended for cold houses	B				
ULTRA BOY: An advance on the more popular Big Boy, according to the suppliers. Earlier, more globular and more productive are the claims	B				
GOLDEN SUNRISE: The usual choice for the gardener who wants a yellow tomato. The fruits are medium-sized with a distinctive taste	N				
GOLDEN BOY: This variety is basically a Beefsteak tomato, but the skin is yellow. The fruits are very large and the texture is meaty	N				
TIGERELLA: An oddity — the fruits bear tiger stripes of red and yellow when mature. The yields are good and so is the flavour	N				

O *Ordinary variety*
F₁ *F₁ hybrid variety*
B *Beefsteak variety*
N *Novelty variety*

TOMATO, OUTDOOR

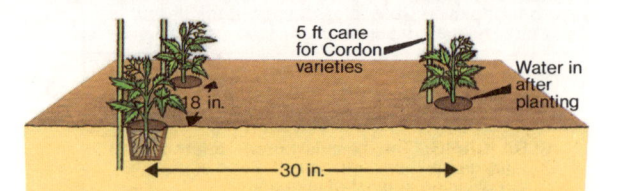

Outdoor tomatoes are not for everyone — in many areas this crop is unreliable and tomatoes need the protection of a greenhouse. But if you live in a mild area and you have a spot which is protected from the wind then you can expect a satisfactory crop in most summers. Choose a spot in front of a south-facing wall if you can. The outdoor crop is basically easier to grow than the indoor one, especially if you choose a Bush variety. Still, it is not an easy crop — regular attention is required. Remember to choose a variety recommended for growing outdoors and make sure that the soil is both free-draining and rich in humus. The tips of Cordon varieties must be removed whilst the plants are still quite small — failure to do so will prevent the tomatoes from ripening.

Choose pot-grown seedlings which are dark green, sturdy and about 8 in. high. Plant out into growing bags, pots or the vegetable plot when the flowers of the first truss are beginning to open — set the top of the soil ball just below the surface.

Loosely tie a Cordon variety to the cane. Pinch out side shoots when they are about 1 in. long. Remove yellowing leaves as the season progresses, but never overdo deleafing.

Water regularly in dry weather — if using growing bags you must water at the recommended frequency. Feed regularly. When small fruits have developed on the 4th truss remove tip at 2 leaves above this truss.

Harvesting

Follow the rules set for greenhouse tomatoes — see page 50.

Types

CORDON varieties

These varieties are grown as single stems and they have to be trimmed and supported. As described above, the stem is stopped after the 4th truss has set so as to hasten ripening before the autumn frosts. There are many red varieties, varying in size from giants to bite-sized fruits, and there are also yellow and striped tomatoes.

AILSA CRAIG
ALICANTE
GOLDEN SUNRISE

Some greenhouse varieties can be grown outdoors. See page 51 for details of these dual-purpose varieties

HARBINGER
MONEYMAKER
TIGERELLA

BUSH varieties

These varieties make outdoor tomato growing much easier. They are either bushes 1–2½ ft high or creeping plants less than 9 in. tall. They do not require supporting, trimming or stopping, and are excellent for cloche culture. One drawback is that the fruits tend to be hidden, which makes harvesting more difficult than with Cordon varieties. Straw or plastic sheeting must be laid around the plants as many fruits are at ground level.

Calendar

The standard time for sowing seed under glass is in late March or early April. The young plants are hardened off during May and planted out in early June, or late May if the weather is favourable and the danger of frost has passed. Plants to be grown under cloches are planted out in the middle of May.

Under average conditions the first tomatoes will be ready for picking in mid August.

	JAN	FEB	MAR	APR	MAY	JUN	JUL	AUG	SEP	OCT	NOV	DEC
Recommended Sowing & Planting Time												
Actual Sowing & Planting Dates												
Expected Picking Time												
Actual Picking Dates												

For key to symbols — see page 7

Varieties

Variety	Type	Variety grown	Yield, flavour & notes for next year	Expected yield
GARDENER'S DELIGHT: Bite-sized tomatoes with a superb tangy flavour. Trusses are long and heavy. This old favourite can be grown under glass	C			
SWEET 100: Another outdoor/indoor variety — over a hundred cherry-sized fruits can be picked from one plant. Flavour is excellent	C			
SMALL FRY: Still another variety producing long ropes of small tomatoes. An outdoor/indoor variety with good disease resistance	C			
MARMANDE: Quite different to the ones above — the fruits are large, fleshy and irregular. These are the well-known 'Continental' tomatoes	C			
GEMINI: Claimed to mature 10–20 days before other outdoor varieties. Can succeed in cold summers. Fruits are medium-sized	C			
OUTDOOR GIRL: An excellent choice for outdoors — very early, high yields and good flavour. Fruits are slightly ribbed. A reliable variety	C			
RONACLAVE: Another good choice — few outdoor Cordon varieties are better. Crops early and heavily — excellent disease resistance. Fruits are large	C			
THE AMATEUR: The most popular but not the best of the Bush tomatoes. A heavy cropper producing medium-sized tomatoes	B			4 lb per plant
RED ALERT: A recent introduction which has become popular. Very early, bearing small fruits with an excellent flavour. Compact growth habit	B			
SPARTAN: Earlier and more compact than most Bush varieties — fruits are medium-sized and sweet. Not in many catalogues.	B			
ALFRESCO: A vigorous Bush tomato — growth habit is spreading and the yields are very high. Not an early variety	B			
SLEAFORD ABUNDANCE: Despite the small amount of leaf borne by this variety the crop is remarkably heavy for a Bush tomato	B			
TORNADO: A splendid new variety. Compact, very early and remarkably long-suffering in poor weather. Foliage is sparse but crops are heavy	B			
ROMA: Try this one for something different. Fruits are long and plum-shaped. Very meaty — good for soups and bottling	B			
TINY TIM: A dwarf variety which you can plant in a windowbox. The cherry-like fruits are bright red and almost seedless	B			
PIXIE: This small plant requires staking. The fruits are small and the flavour is good. Disappointing in indifferent summers	B			
TOTEM: A British-bred variety which is recommended for growing in pots or growing bags outdoors. Dwarf, compact and early ripening	B			

C Cordon variety
B Bush variety

VEGETABLES A–Z

TURNIP

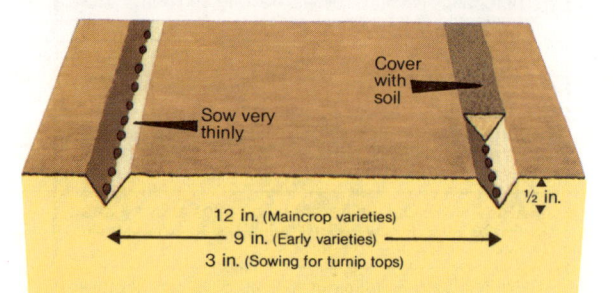

Turnips are an easy-to-grow and quick-maturing crop. The Early varieties are pulled when the roots are still young and are used in salads or for cooking — they cannot be stored. Round is not the only shape for these Earlies — there are also flat ones. There is a range of colours in the globular Maincrop varieties which are sown in summer for cropping and storage in autumn. Early turnips are more demanding than Maincrop varieties for good soil and good growing conditions.

Sow very thinly. Cover with soil. ½ in.
12 in. (Maincrop varieties)
9 in. (Early varieties)
3 in. (Sowing for turnip tops)

Harvesting

Pull Early varieties when the roots are golf ball size for eating raw or snooker ball size for cooking. Begin lifting Maincrop turnips with a fork in October — in most areas you can leave the roots in the soil and lift as required. In cold and wet areas harvest the crop in early November, twist off the leaves and store the roots between layers of peat in a stout box.

Thin out turnips when seedlings are large enough to handle. Do this in stages until plants are 9 in. (Maincrop varieties) or 5 in. (Early varieties) apart. Do not thin turnips grown for tops.

Hoe as necessary. Spray with Crop Saver at the first signs of flea beetle damage.

Water in dry weather — failure to do so can result in small, woody and cracked roots.

Varieties

Variety	Type	Shape & colour	Variety grown	Yield, flavour & notes for next year	Expected yield
PURPLE-TOP MILAN: A popular Early — flat and reddish on top. Matures very quickly	E				Early varieties: 7 lb from a 10 ft row / Maincrop varieties: 12 lb from a 10 ft row
MILAN WHITE FORCING: Another Early — choose this one for growing under cloches or in frames	E				
SNOWBALL: The popular globular Early — quick-growing, white-fleshed and reliable	E				
TOKYO CROSS: Can be sown May–early September for turnips 6 weeks later	E				
RED GLOBE: A medium-sized Early. The flesh is white — the skin is red-topped	E				
GOLDEN BALL: The most popular and perhaps best of the Maincrops. Yellow-fleshed	M				
MANCHESTER MARKET: A typical green-topped variety — excellent for winter storage	M				
ARCA: Another green-top — reliable, white-fleshed and medium-sized	M				
GREEN-TOP STONE: The variety recommended for use as spring greens. Roots are large	M				
MODEL WHITE: The only all-white Maincrop you are likely to find. Good flavour	M				
ORANGE JELLY: Sown as an alternative to swedes where the latter crop is difficult to grow	M				

E *Early variety*
M *Maincrop variety*

Calendar

Early turnips: Sow Milan White Forcing under cloches in February and other Early varieties outdoors during March–June for a May–September crop.

Maincrop turnips: Sow Maincrop varieties in mid July–mid August for cropping and storage from mid October onwards.

Turnip tops: Sow a Maincrop variety in August or September for spring greens in March and April.

	JAN	FEB	MAR	APR	MAY	JUN	JUL	AUG	SEP	OCT	NOV	DEC
Recommended Sowing Time												
Actual Sowing Dates												
Expected Lifting Time				TOPS ONLY								
Actual Lifting Dates												

For key to symbols — see page 7

CHAPTER 3
CARE

BUYING SEED

When you buy a packet of seeds your interests are protected by law – there are standards of purity and germination capacity, but you must still choose carefully. You will find all the popular favourites in your local garden centre or shop, and most of these varieties have stood the test of time. For more unusual varieties you will have to turn to the mail order seed catalogues. Most of the varieties offered for sale are open-pollinated seed, which means that no specialist hybridisation has been carried out. F_1 hybrid seed is the product of crossing two pure-bred parents. Vigour and uniformity are generally increased, but so is the price.

Suppliers

Name	Comments
Local	
Mail Order	

INTERCROPPING

Remember the value of intercropping when drawing up your vegetable plot plan. Between adjacent rows of notorious slow developers such as brussels sprouts, leeks, parsnips etc a row of a fast-maturing crop is sown which will be harvested in summer before the prime crop needs the space. Popular intercroppers are radish, early peas, early carrots and dwarf lettuce. The intercropping vegetable must not make the space between the rows too narrow — if necessary widen the row spacing of the prime crop.

GROWING UNDER CLOCHES

The sowing or planting of many vegetables under cloches can be carried out weeks earlier than on unprotected ground. This means that harvesting can take place much earlier and that will be when shop prices are high. Half-hardy crops such as capsicums can be grown successfully in less than favourable areas and leafy vegetables in winter are protected from the worst of the weather.

Choose your cloches wisely. Match the height to the expected size of the plants as the leaves should not touch the sides. Tent cloches are suitable for small plants, but you will need barn cloches for larger ones. Plastic has the benefits of lightness, safety and cheapness, but glass offers maximum clarity, stability and heat retention. To cover large areas cheaply use a plastic tunnel cloche made from wire hoops and polythene sheeting.

Provide ventilation by leaving gaps between the cloches, not by leaving the ends open. There is no need to remove the cloches before watering — the water will run down the sides and into the soil. Make sure the cloches are firmly anchored into the ground and wash the surface if it becomes grimy. Remember to increase ventilation for a few days to harden off the plants before removing their protection.

MANURING

This is the start of the gardening year. In autumn or early winter bulky organic matter is spread over the soil surface at the rate of 1 barrowload per 10 sq.yd. The area chosen should be for crops other than roots or brassicas — see page 2. This layer of organic matter is then dug into the soil. It is vital that this manuring routine is carried out so that part of the plot is enriched each year until the whole area has been treated.

Manure or fertilizer — the age-old argument. Actually there is nothing to argue about. The role of bulky organic matter is to make the *soil structure* good enough to support a vigorous and healthy crop. The role of fertilizer is to provide the *plants* with enough nutrients to ensure that they reach their full potential.

The basic (and best) materials to use are well-rotted animal manure or garden compost. Both contain the colloidal gums released by dead bacteria during the composting process. These gums produce soil crumbs and improve friability. The fibrous organic materials (peat, bark etc) are long lasting but are also less effective — they have a purely physical effect in opening up the soil and do not promote crumb formation.

Manuring Record

Notes

THINNING

Despite the often-repeated recommendation to sow thinly you will usually find that the emerged seedlings are too close together. Thinning is necessary, and this is a job to be tackled as soon as the plants are large enough to handle — delay will result in spindly, weak plants which never fully recover. The soil should be moist — water if necessary. Hold down the earth around the unwanted seedling with one hand and pull the plant up with the other. If the seedlings are too close together to allow this technique, merely nip off the top growth of the unwanted ones and leave the roots in the soil. After thinning, firm the soil around the remaining seedlings and water gently. This thinning is often done in stages before the final spacing is reached.

TRANSPLANTING

Transplanting involves moving seedlings to their permanent quarters. These transplants may have been raised in a seed bed in the garden, bought from a reliable supplier or grown under glass in pots or trays of compost. It is a temptation to lift thinnings in an overcrowded row of seedlings in the garden and plant them elsewhere, but you must remember that transplanting is not suitable for all vegetables. It is firmly recommended for most brassicas, acceptable for some popular crops such as peas and beans and definitely not recommended for many others such as lettuce and root crops. The rule is to check first. Water both the seedlings and the site where they are to be planted on the day before transplanting. Use a trowel (or a dibber for brassicas) to set the plants at the depth they were in the seed bed or pot. Firm the soil around the plants and water in to settle the roots. Transplanting is a critical time in the plant's life. Cold, wet soil can be fatal and so can late frosts for half-hardy vegetables. Water if there is a dry spell after planting and provide protection if birds are a habitual nuisance.

MULCHING

Mulching is an in-season method of manuring. A 1–2 in. layer of peat, well-rotted compost or leaf mould is spread between the young plants once they are established in spring. Cultivate and water the surface to make sure that it is moist, weed-free and friable before application. The mulch will reduce water loss, increase nutrient content, improve soil structure and suppress weeds.

EARTHING-UP

There are several reasons for earthing-up — the drawing of soil towards and around the stems. Potatoes are earthed-up to avoid the tubers being exposed to light. When the haulm is about 9 in. high a draw hoe is used to pile loose soil against the stems to form a flat-topped ridge. The greens (broccoli, kale, brussels sprouts etc) are earthed-up for a different reason — soil is drawn up around the stems of well-developed plants to improve anchorage against high winds.

The stems of celery and leek are blanched (see page 27) by earthing-up. This begins with celery when it is about 1 ft high — with leeks this is done in stages, the height being increased a little at a time by drawing dry soil around the stems.

FEEDING

There are a number of nutrients which are vital for vegetables — nitrogen for leaf growth, phosphates for root development and potash for strengthening resistance to disease and poor conditions. This group is required in relatively large amounts and compound fertilizers contain all three. You will find a statement of the nutrient content on the package.

One of the most important uses for compound fertilizers is to provide a **base dressing** just before sowing or planting. A granular or powder formulation is used, and Growmore is the old favourite. There are a few, such as Back to Nature fertilizer, which are based entirely on minerals and organics.

Crops which take some time to mature will need one or more **top dressings** during the growing season. These can be in powder or granular form, but you must take great care to keep such dressings off the leaves. It is better to use a soluble fertilizer such as Bio Plant Food. For maximum yields the top dressing should be balanced to the needs of the particular crop and its stage of growth. A nitrogen-rich one (e.g Leaf Maker) is used to promote leaf and/or stem growth. This is changed to a potash-rich one (e.g Flower Maker) when fruit stimulation rather than leaf growth is required.

The big three (nitrogen, phosphates and potash) are not the only vital elements. Magnesium is required in moderate amounts and a number of others (manganese, iron, molybdenum, boron, etc) are needed in trace amounts. Manuring adds some to the soil — overliming and waterlogging lock them up. If you have suffered from deficiencies in the past, use MultiTonic around the plants.

Feeding Record

Date	Feed	Notes

WATERING

A prolonged dry spell can result in a small crop or even no crop at all. Heavy rain after drought causes the splitting of tomatoes and roots. Effective watering is the answer, and it is an art you must learn. Unfortunately, watering is usually dealt with very briefly in most handbooks on vegetable growing, but without adequate irrigation many crops will give disastrous results in a dry season.

The first step is to incorporate adequate organic matter into the soil — this increases the water-holding capacity. Next, the top 9 in. of soil should be thoroughly and evenly moist but not waterlogged at sowing or planting time. Finally, put down a mulch (see page 56) in late spring.

You will have done all you can to ensure a good moisture reservoir in your soil — the rest is up to the weather. If there is a prolonged dry spell then water will be necessary, especially for tomatoes, cucumbers, marrows, beans, peas, celery and onions.

The rule is to water the soil gently and thoroughly every 7 days when the weather is dry during the critical period. This is between flowering and full pod development for peas and beans, and from seedling to maturity for leaf crops. Apply 2 gallons per square yard when **overall watering**, and try to water in the morning rather than at midday or in the evening. Remember to water slowly and close to the base of the plants. A watering can is often used but you really do need a hosepipe if watering is not to be a prolonged chore. One of the most effective methods of watering is to use lay-flat perforated tubing between the rows. Simple ... but expensive. Where there is a limited number of large plants to deal with, you would do better to use a technique known as **point watering**. This involves inserting an empty plant pot or creating a depression in the soil around each stem. Water is then poured into the pot or depression.

The main reason for failure or disappointment with growing bags is due to trying to follow the traditional technique used for watering the garden. Keeping the compost in a growing bag properly moist is a different technique, and you should follow the maker's instructions carefully.

Watering Record

Date	Notes

WEEDING

There is no single miracle cure for the weed problem — there are a number of tasks you will have to carry out. The first one begins before the crop is sown — at digging time remove all the roots of perennial weeds and bury small annual weeds by inverting each spadeful of soil. If the allotment or vegetable plot has been neglected and is a sea of grass and other weeds then you have a problem on your hands. The best plan is to spray with glyphosate before soil preparation.

However thoroughly you remove weeds before sowing or planting, additional weeds will appear among the growing plants. Hoeing is the basic technique — it must be carried out at regular intervals in order to keep annual weeds in constant check and to starve out the underground parts of perennial ones. Keep away from the stems and do not go deeper than an inch below the surface.

Chemicals have a part to play, but must be used with care as they cannot distinguish between friend and foe. Use Weedol to burn off weed growth between plants — paint leaves of perennial weeds with glyphosate.

Weeding Record

Notes

STORING

Most of the vegetables we grow are eaten shortly after picking or lifting, and that is the ideal time. Nearly all vegetables can be kept for a few days or even a week or two in the refrigerator, but it we take growing seriously then there will be times when long-term storage will be necessary. With beans there is always a sudden glut, and it is far better to pick them at the tender stage for storage rather than trying to extend the harvest period to the time when they will be tough and stringy. Maincrops of roots are generally lifted in autumn for storage indoors as layers between sand or peat (beetroots, carrots, etc) or in sacks (potatoes) in a frost-free shed or garage. It is possible to let the vegetable plot act as the vegetable store for some roots — swedes, parsnips and turnips can be lifted as required.

Long-term storage has been completely transformed by the advent of the home freezer. This is the ideal storage method for so many vegetables, including the leafy ones which cannot be kept satisfactorily by any other method. The routine is to blanch, cool, drain and then freeze.

CARE

page 57

PESTS & DISEASES

PEA & BEAN WEEVIL — Leaf edges notched | Pea, Bean

RED SPIDER MITE — Leaves turn mottled, grey or brown. Fine web and minute insects on undersurface | Bean, Tomato, Cucumber (under glass)

WHITE TIP — End of leaves turn white | Leek

PEA MILDEW — White powdery mould on leaves and stems | Pea

DOWNY MILDEW — Leaves yellowish, grey or purple mould on undersurface | Cabbage family, Lettuce, Onion

LEAF MINER — White blisters on leaf, containing a maggot | Celery

PEA MOTH — Small, white maggots in Peas | Pea

WHITEFLY — Tiny white moth-like insects | Cabbage family, Tomato

THRIPS — Pods distorted | Pea, Bean

BLACKFLY — Small plump black insects | Bean, Beet

GREENFLY — Small, plump insects — green-grey, mauve or white | Cabbage family, Lettuce, Pea, Carrot

TOMATO LEAF MOULD — Yellow blotches on top of leaves, purplish patches on undersurface | Tomato (under glass)

CABBAGE CATERPILLAR — Holes eaten in leaves | Cabbage family

BLIGHT — Brown blotches on leaves | Potato, Tomato

GREY MOULD — Fluffy grey or white mould on leaves and stems | General vegetable disease

EELWORM — Tubers small; plants small and weak. Poor root growth | Potato

SLUGS & SNAILS — Holes in leaves and stems | General vegetable pests

WIREWORM MILLEPEDE — Tubers holed | Potato

CUTWORM — Stem eaten through at ground level | Cabbage family, Lettuce

WIREWORM, LEATHERJACKET, CHAFER GRUB, MILLEPEDE, SLUGS & SNAILS — Underground stems and roots eaten | General vegetable pests

SCAB — Brown corky scabs on tubers | Potato

WART DISEASE — Warty outgrowths on tubers | Potato

BLIGHT — Soft patches on tubers. Tubers rot in store | Potato

ROOT APHID — White insects on roots. Plants stop growing | Lettuce

CABBAGE ROOT FLY, CARROT FLY, ONION FLY — Small white maggots in root | Cabbage, Carrot, Onion (bulb)

CABBAGE GALL WEEVIL — Swollen root, maggots inside | Cabbage family

CLUB ROOT — Swollen root, no maggots inside | Cabbage family

page 58

1. TREAT PROMPTLY IF TROUBLE CAN BE CURED OR CHECKED

Pest	Treatment	Notes
WHITEFLY	CROP SAVER / LIQUID DERRIS / MALATHION GREENFLY KILLER / HEXYL / LONG-LAST / SPRAYDAY / FENITROTHION	Repeat spraying is essential
RED SPIDER MITE		Maintain damp atmosphere under glass
PEA THRIPS		Keep watch in hot, dry weather
GREENFLY		Spray when first colonies appear
BLACKFLY		Spray when first colonies appear
SMALL CATERPILLARS		Spray serious attacks — otherwise hand pick
LEAF MINER		Pick and destroy mined leaves
OTHER CATERPILLARS		Spray serious attacks — otherwise hand pick
PEA & BEAN WEEVIL		Hoe around plants in April–May
PEA MOTH		Spray 7–10 days after flowers open
CABBAGE ROOT FLY, CARROT FLY, ONION FLY, CUTWORM, WIREWORM, MILLEPEDE, LEATHERJACKET, CHAFER GRUB	BROMOPHOS will guard your plants against these pests but correct timing is very important — follow the directions on the drum. Sprinkle the granules evenly over the soil surface at the recommended rate and then rake in ligntly. Unlike some soil pest killers, BROMOPHOS does not taint root crops	
ROOT APHID	Apply BROMOPHOS (see above) or water with spray-strength MALATHION	
SLUGS & SNAILS	SLUG PELLETS based on metaldehyde are the traditional method of killing slugs and snails	
CABBAGE GALL WEEVIL	BROMOPHOS (see above) reduces risk — treatment not worthwhile	

Disease	Control
POTATO & TOMATO BLIGHT, DOWNY MILDEW, LEEK WHITE TIP	Spray with DITHANE as soon as the first symptoms are seen — repeat every fortnight as necessary. To prevent blight in a wet summer apply the first spray in early July
BEAN CHOCOLATE SPOT (dark brown spots on leaves), CELERY LEAF SPOT (brown spots on leaves), PEA MILDEW, GREY MOULD, TOMATO LEAF MOULD	Spray with SUPERCARB as soon as the first symptoms are seen — read the leaflet for precise instructions. Repeat as necessary
CLUB ROOT	Make sure the soil is adequately limed and well drained. Before planting dip roots in SUPERCARB solution or CALOMEL DUST paste
POTATO SCAB	No treatment. In future dig in compost but do not lime before planting

2. TAKE THE RECOMMENDED ACTION IF TROUBLE IS INCURABLE

POTATO EELWORM remains in the soil for a long time. Destroy plants and do not grow potatoes or tomatoes on the land for at least 6 years.

POTATO WART DISEASE must be notified to the Ministry of Agriculture. Destroy plants — in future grow a resistant variety.

SOFT ROT of potatoes, turnips etc results in slimy, evil-smelling roots. Burn affected produce — in future take care not to injure roots at lifting time.

VIRUS diseases can be serious on the vegetable plot — potatoes, tomatoes and cucumbers are some of the crops at risk. There is no cure — lift and burn.

3. CONSULT THE VEGETABLE EXPERT IF PEST IS NOT ILLUSTRATED

The vegetable troubles described on these two pages include most of the serious pests and diseases. There are many other problems which can occur, and some of these are nutritional or cultural disorders rather than the result of insect or fungal attack. Examples include bull-necked onions, forked carrots, bolted lettuces and blown brussels sprouts. Some of the cultural problems are shown overleaf. If your problem is not shown on page 58 or 61 consult a copy of The Vegetable Expert.

CULTURAL CONTROL OF PESTS & DISEASES

- **Choose wisely.** Read about the crop before you buy — don't rely solely on the seed packet. Make sure that the variety is suitable for the chosen sowing date and don't leave your purchase to the last minute — many select varieties sell out early. Sometimes you will need to buy seedlings instead of seeds for transplanting into the plot. Choose carefully — the plants should be sturdy, free from diseases and discoloration and there should be a good root system. Here you must leave it to the last minute because there should be as little delay as possible between buying and planting.

- **Prepare the ground properly.** Good drainage is vital — a plant in waterlogged soil is likely to succumb to root-rotting organisms. Follow the rules for the correct way to manure, feed and lime the soil — remember that vegetables vary widely in their soil needs. The time for digging is autumn or early winter if you plan to sow in spring.

- **Get rid of weeds and rubbish.** Weeds rob the plants of water, food, space and light. Rubbish, like weeds, can be a breeding ground for pests and diseases.

- **Rotate your crops.** Soil troubles and nutrient deficiencies can build up if you grow the same crop year after year on the same site. Crop rotation is necessary for successful vegetable production — see the rules on page 2.

- **Avoid overcrowding.** Sow seed thinly. Thin the seedlings as soon after germination as practical — overcrowding leads to crippled plants and high disease risk. Do not leave thinnings on the plot — put them on the compost heap or burn if instructed to do so.

- **Get rid of badly infected plants.** Do not leave sources of infection in the garden. Remove and destroy untreatable plants when this book tells you to do so.

- **Feed and water correctly.** Some plant troubles are due to incorrect feeding and soil moisture problems. Use a balanced fertilizer containing nitrogen, phosphates and potash — follow the instructions. Never let the roots get dry but daily sprinklings instead of a good soaking may do more harm than good.

CHEMICAL CONTROL OF PESTS & DISEASES

BEFORE SPRAYING: Choose the product carefully. Make sure that the problem is mentioned on the label. Insecticides should be used at the first sign of attack. A systemic insecticide enters the sap stream and so can reach insects which are hidden from the spray. Fungicides prevent rather than cure diseases, so early spraying is vital. Systemic fungicides enter the sap stream. Always read the label carefully and follow the instructions and precautions.

SPRAYING: Choose a day which is neither sunny nor windy, and choose a time in summer which is late in the day so that bees will not be harmed. Make up the spray as directed — never use equipment which has contained weedkillers. Use a fine forceful spray to cover the top and underside of the foliage — continue until the liquid starts to run off the leaves. Try to keep all sprays off the skin. If splashes occur, wash the affected area immediately.

AFTER SPRAYING: Wash out equipment thoroughly. Do this straight away — do not leave the chemical to dry inside the nozzle. Wash your hands and face if the label tells you to do so. Do not pour leftover spray into a bottle for use next time — you should make up a fresh batch of solution each time you wish to treat your plants. Store containers in a safe place away from pets and children. Never transfer chemicals into bottles — throw old containers into the dustbin after disposing of the contents safely.

Spraying Record

Date	Problem	Pesticide used	Comments

GENERAL DISORDERS

WIND
Wind is often ignored as a danger, yet a cold east wind in spring can kill in the same way as frost. More frequently the effect is the browning of leaf margins. Another damaging effect is wind rock, which can lead to rotting of the roots.

FROST
A severe late frost will kill half-hardy vegetables. The shoots of asparagus and potatoes are blackened, but healthy shoots appear after the frosts have passed. The general symptoms of moderate damage are yellow patches or marginal browning of the leaves. The basic rule is to avoid sowing or planting before the recommended time unless you can provide protection. If your garden is on a sloping site, open part of the lower boundary to air movement so as to prevent the creation of a 'frost pocket'.

TOO LITTLE WATER
The first sign is a dull leaf colour, and this is followed by wilting of the foliage. Discoloration becomes more pronounced and growth is checked. Lettuces become leathery, roots turn woody and some plants run to seed. Flowers and young fruit may drop off. If water shortage continues, leaves turn brown and fall, and the plant dies. Avoid trouble by incorporating organic matter, by watering thoroughly and by mulching.

TOO MUCH WATER
Waterlogging affects the plant in two ways. Root development is crippled by the shortage of air in the soil. The root system becomes shallow, and also ineffective as the root hairs die. Leaves often turn pale and growth is stunted. The second serious effect is the stimulation of root-rotting diseases. Good drainage is therefore essential, and this calls for thorough autumn digging. Incorporate plenty of organic matter into heavy soil — the correct timing for humus addition depends on the crop being grown.

HEAVY RAIN FOLLOWING DROUGHT
The outer skin of many vegetables hardens under drought conditions, and when heavy rain or watering takes place the sudden increase in growth stretches and then splits the skin. This results in the splitting of tomatoes, potatoes and roots. Avoid by watering before the soil dries out.

TOO LITTLE PLANT FOOD
The major plant foods are nitrogen, phosphates and potash, and a vigorous crop acts as a heavy drain on the soil's resources. Nitrogen shortage leads to stunted growth, pale leaves and occasional red discoloration. Potash shortage leads to poor disease resistance, marginal leaf scorch, and produce with poor cooking and keeping qualities. Before sowing or planting apply a complete fertilizer, such as Growmore fertilizer, containing all the major nutrients.
One or more dressings should be applied to the growing plants. Backward vegetables are helped by a leaf-feeding fertilizer such as Fillip.

SHADE
In a small garden deep shade may be the major problem. Straggling soft growth is produced and the leaves tend to be small. Such plants are prone to attack by pests and diseases. Grow leaf and root types rather than fruit and pod vegetables.

TRACE ELEMENT SHORTAGE
Vegetables often show deficiency symptoms such as yellowing between the veins and leaf scorch. The most important trace elements are magnesium, manganese, iron, molybdenum and boron. Make sure the soil is well supplied with compost or manure. If your soil is known to have a trace element deficiency problem, undoubtedly the best answer is to water the ground early in the season with MultiTonic — a product containing all the trace elements required by plants in Britain.

TOO LITTLE ORGANIC MATTER
The soil must be in good heart and this calls for liberal amounts of organic matter. Not all materials are suitable; peat may increase aeration and water retention but the need is for an active source of humus. Good garden compost and well-rotted manure are ideal. Timing is all-important — look up individual crops in this book for details.

CARE

CHAPTER 4
DIARY

JANUARY

A quiet time in the vegetable garden, but you can dig if the soil is not too wet. Rhubarb can be planted now — cover established crowns with an upturned bucket to force an early crop. A few crops may be sown — leeks, onions for exhibition and tomatoes for a heated greenhouse are started this month under glass indoors — radishes can be sown outdoors under cloches.

FEBRUARY

A busier time than January, but frosty weather may make outdoor work impossible. Peas, broad beans, radishes and turnips can be sown under cloches, and greenhouse cucumbers are started indoors. Shallot planting can begin and now is the time to buy seed potatoes and set them in trays to encourage sprouting. Inspect plants for wind damage — stake if necessary.

MARCH

The vegetable year starts in earnest this month, but do not rush to sow all the early-season vegetables if the soil is still very wet and cold. March is the peak time for sowing broad beans, brussels sprouts, leeks, onions, parsnips, early peas and early turnips. It is also the month for sowing various crops under glass — capsicum, celeriac, celery, tomatoes and cucumbers.

Plant early potatoes and onion sets. Summer cabbage can be sown under cloches and so can early carrots. Top dress spring cabbage with fertilizer. Plant tomato and cucumber seedlings in pots or growing bags in a heated greenhouse.

APRIL

A peak month for sowing seed outdoors. Now is the time to put in broad beans, leaf beet, beetroot, broccoli, brussels sprouts, summer and winter cabbage, carrots, cauliflower, lettuce, peas, radishes, spinach and turnips. Finish sowing leeks, onions and parsnips.

Complete the planting of potatoes, globe artichokes and asparagus — start cutting asparagus on established beds. Sow french beans under cloches in the south, and in warmer districts plant out tomato seedlings in a cold greenhouse. A number of vegetables can be harvested this month, including late broccoli, turnip tops, spring cabbage and rhubarb. Kale and leek harvesting come to an end this month.

MAY

A busy time in the vegetable garden — sowing, planting and hoeing. Sow french beans, runner beans, beetroot, carrots, chicory, outdoor cucumber, kale, marrows, courgettes, maincrop peas, mangetout, radishes, spinach and swedes. Finish sowing broad beans, leaf beet, summer and winter cabbage, broccoli and cauliflower.

It is planting time for a number of crops — brussels sprouts, celeriac, celery, capsicum, summer cabbage and tomatoes in a cold greenhouse. Prepare the planting sites for courgettes, marrows and outdoor cucumbers — harvest early-sown lettuce and radishes.

JUNE

June is an important planting month rather than a seed-sowing one, although successional sowings of lettuces, french beans, radishes and peas continue. Finish sowing beetroot, carrots and swedes.

Vegetables for planting out include broccoli, early potatoes, brussels sprouts, sweet corn, winter cabbage, capsicum, cauliflower, celery, celeriac, leeks, courgettes, marrows and outdoor tomatoes and cucumbers — a lengthy list! Finish cutting asparagus — begin picking early-sown broad beans. Keep the plot watered if a dry spell occurs — keep watch for pest attacks. Damp down the floor and staging of the greenhouse to maintain a moist atmosphere. Apply shading to the glass.

JULY

There are numerous vegetables to harvest this month — broad beans, early-sown french beans, beetroot, greenhouse cucumbers and tomatoes, courgettes, shallots, onions, lettuce, peas, radishes, onions etc.

Sow chicory, winter radishes and maincrop turnips — continue planting lettuce and peas. Finish planting broccoli, winter cabbage, cauliflower, kale and leeks. Hoe as necessary — spray against cabbage white caterpillar and potato blight if attacks are seen. Water during a dry spell — feed with a liquid fertilizer. Pinch out side shoots on cordon tomato plants.

AUGUST

Sow winter spinach, short-rooted carrots, lettuce for an early winter crop, japanese onions, winter radishes, maincrop turnips, salad onions and spring cabbage.

There are lots of cultural jobs this month — watering, hoeing, spraying, blanching celery etc, but August is a peak month for gathering in the crops — broad beans, french beans, runner beans, leaf beet, beetroot, green broccoli, summer cabbage, capsicum, carrots, summer cauliflower, greenhouse and outdoor cucumbers and tomatoes, marrows, courgettes, onions, shallots, peas, early potatoes and globe artichokes. It is essential to harvest at the right stage — see Vegetables A-Z section.

DIARY

SEPTEMBER

Many of the vegetables which could be gathered in August can also be harvested this month, but there are additional ones — sweet corn, celery, autumn cauliflower, brussels sprouts raised under cloches, early savoys, red cabbage and early leeks. Maincrop potatoes and carrots are lifted for storage this month. Pick tomatoes from outdoor plants and bring indoors for ripening. Plant spring cabbage.

Sow lettuce under glass for a midwinter crop or outdoors in mild districts for a spring crop. Remove shading from greenhouse glass. Cut down asparagus fern.

OCTOBER

Sow peas under cloches for a May–June crop — if you live in a mild district you can sow lettuce under cloches for spring use. Finish planting spring cabbage.

This is the great harvest month. Finish cropping french beans, runner beans, marrows, potatoes, summer cabbage, sweet corn, maincrop carrots, maincrop beetroot, greenhouse tomatoes and cucumbers, summer-sown lettuce, winter radishes and turnips. Start harvesting swedes, maincrop turnips, brussels sprouts and winter cabbage.

NOVEMBER

Cleaning up starts in earnest — begin digging. Sow broad beans in a sheltered spot and lettuce under cloches. Force chicory and cut back globe artichokes.

Harvest brussels sprouts, winter cabbage, summer-sown carrots, celeriac, celery, leeks, parsnips, swedes and turnips. November is the last month for gathering leaf beet and autumn cauliflower. Put together your seed order for next year — don't wait until the last minute.

DECEMBER

Continue digging if weather permits. Check over your tools and oil if necessary. In many gardens there is very little to gather in December apart from brussels sprouts, but in the well-stocked plot there are many vegetables to gather. These include summer-sown carrots, summer-sown lettuce under cloches, winter spinach, swedes, turnips, winter cabbage, savoys, celery, kale, chicory and leeks.

Acknowledgements

The author wishes to acknowledge the painstaking work of Gill Jackson, Jane Llewelyn and John Woodbridge. Grateful acknowledgement is also made to Constance Barry, Joan Hessayon, Linda Fensom and Angelina Gibbs. Mike Standage and Yvon Still prepared the paintings for this book.

CHAPTER 1
GROWING VEGETABLES AT HOME

The greate[...]
the past fe[...]
vegetable g[...]
now eagerly [...]
Gone are the [...] ...adays
we have sh[...] ...the favourite varieties well
before the end of the season.

Why? The rapid increase in shop prices is obviously the most important reason. The textbook advice not to bother with 'cheap' vegetables such as potatoes has an out-of-date ring to it. Inflation has turned a healthy hobby for the few into a money-saving activity for the majority of gardeners. The increasing popularity of home freezers is another important factor; the once-annoying gluts of beans, broccoli and brussels sprouts can now be frozen for later use.

So the vegetable plot and the freezer enable you to produce at home what you used to buy from the shops. But there is more to it than that. You can pick at the peak of tenderness and flavour, not when yields are highest. You can also serve vegetables within an hour or two of picking, and with sweet corn, peas, beans, asparagus etc. this means a new flavour experience for you. Nor need it stop there, for you can grow vegetables which never appear in the shops or you can grow top-flavour varieties of ordinary vegetables which farmers never grow.

The choice is up to you, and so is the size of your vegetable garden. It takes a well-run plot of 100 sq. yards to keep one person in vegetables (except maincrop potatoes) for a year. At the other end of the scale a few tubs filled with potting compost on a balcony can provide fresh tomatoes, french beans, courgettes and new potatoes. Either way, there is the joy of growing your own.

BASIC RULES

○ DIG EARLY
Don't try to dig and make a seed bed in one operation. The time for digging is during a dry spell in late autumn or early winter if you plan to sow in the spring. Then the frosts will produce a crumbly surface if you leave it in a rough condition. In early spring the soil will become workable – moist but not sticky. Now is the time to make a seed bed. Firm down the surface with your feet and level it off with a rake.

○ BUY GOOD SEEDS & PLANTS
Always obtain good quality seed, and don't leave it to the last minute in these days of seed shortage. Store the packets inside a tin with a tight lid in a cool place. Sometimes you will need to buy seedlings instead of seeds for transplanting into the plot. Choose carefully – the plants should be sturdy, green and with a good root system. Here you *must* leave it to the last minute, because there must be a minimum delay between purchase and planting.

BEFORE SOWING OR PLANTING:
Rake in fertilizer
GROW **ROOT CROPS:** Beetroot, Carrot, Parsnip, Potato, Swede or Turnip

BEFORE SOWING OR PLANTING:
Rake in fertilizer and lime
GROW **BRASSICA CROPS:** Broccoli, Brussels Sprout, Cabbage, Cauliflower or Kale

BEFORE SOWING OR PLANTING:
Dig in manure, compost or peat
GROW **'OTHER' CROPS:** Bean, Celery, Cucumber, Leek, Lettuce, Marrow, Onion, Pea, Radish, Sweet Corn or Tomato

○ ROTATE YOUR CROPS
You should not grow a vegetable in the same spot year after year. If you do then soil troubles will start to build up, and the level of soil nutrients will become unbalanced. Crop rotation is the answer, and the best plan is illustrated here. Not everyone is able to use this, and unfortunately all idea of a rotation is often abandoned. It would be much better to follow a very simple rotation – roots this year, an above-ground crop next year and then back to a root crop.

○ SOW & PLANT AT THE PROPER TIME
Proper timing is extremely important. The calendars in this book will give you approximate times for sowing and planting – soil and weather conditions determine the exact time. The soil must be moist but it must *not* be wet and waterlogged. Sow seeds in drills; broadcasting them over an area makes weeding difficult. Mark the ends of the rows with sticks and remember the basic seed sowing rule – not too early, not too deeply, not too thickly.

○ THIN PROMPTLY & ENSURE RAPID GROWTH
Remove weeds and thin the seedlings as soon after germination as possible. Overcrowding at this early stage can be crippling. Firm the plants after thinning and gently water to settle the disturbed roots. Tenderness and flavour in leaf and many root crops depend on rapid growth, so ensure that the plants receive adequate water and nutrients.

○ SOW NON-STORABLE CROPS LITTLE & OFTEN
Several vegetables, such as lettuce, radish and cabbage, cannot be stored for later use. To avoid gluts and then famines it is necessary to sow a short row every few weeks. A boon for the busy (or lazy) gardener are the 'mixed seed' packets of lettuce, radish etc. offered by many suppliers. The mixture of early- and late-maturing varieties gives a long harvesting period from a single sowing.

○ PICK MOST CROPS EARLY & OFTEN
You may be surprised at some of the harvesting stages recommended in this book – turnips the size of a golf ball and carrots no longer than a finger. But these are the times of peak flavour and tenderness. With some crops, such as marrows, cucumber, peas and beans, it is essential to pick regularly as just a few mature fruits or pods left on the plant can bring cropping to an end.

The Vegetable Plot

Draw in the outline of your plot and the position of the vegetable rows. Write in the name of the first-sown vegetable on the *left* of the row – subsequent crops on the *right*.

Vegetable Grower's Dictionary

BLANCHING
Excluding light from stems of celery, leek, endive etc. to make them more palatable.

BLIND
A plant without a bud at its tip.

BOLTING
Prematurely running to seed.

BRASSICA
Member of the cabbage family.

BROADCAST
Seed spread evenly over an area rather than in drills.

CATCH CROP
Quick-maturing crop grown in the short interval between lifting one maincrop and planting another.

DRILL
A straight and shallow furrow in which seeds are sown.

EARTHING UP
Drawing up soil around the stems of plants.

EYE
An undeveloped growth bud.

F_1 HYBRID SEED
Obtained by crossing 2 true parent strains. Vigour and other properties are increased.

HALF HARDY
A plant which cannot stand frost, but which can be grown outdoors once the danger of frost has passed.

HARDENING OFF
Gradually acclimatising plants grown under glass to the conditions they will have to face outdoors.

HARDY
A plant which can withstand the frosts of a normal winter.

HAULM
Another name for the shoots of some vegetables (peas, beans, potatoes etc.).

IMMUNE
Resistant to a certain disease. Note that immune varieties are not resistant to all diseases.

INTERCROP
A crop grown between rows of another vegetable.

LEGUME
Member of the pea and bean family.

MAINCROP
The varieties and planting times which yield the major harvest of the vegetable and provide the supply for storage.

MULCH
A surface layer of organic matter, used to suppress weeds and conserve moisture.

OPEN
Description of winter weather when it is neither raining nor freezing.

PINCHING OUT
Removing the growing tip of the stem to keep the plant compact or to hasten maturity.

PRICKING OUT
Transplanting a seedling from where it was germinated to another container.

SEED LEAVES
The first leaf, or pair of leaves, after germination.

SET
The fertilization of the flower – the start of fruit development.

SOIL BALL
The mass of roots and soil of a pot-grown plant.

SPIT
The depth of a spade – about 10 in.

SYSTEMIC
A fungicide, insecticide or fertilizer which is able to penetrate the leaves and enter the sap system.

TILTH
The texture of the soil.

TRUE LEAVES
The leaves which appear after the seed leaves and are typical of the plant.

TRUSS
A cluster of fruit at the end of a stem, as in tomatoes.

VARIETY
The popular name for the technical term 'cultivar' (= cultivated variety).

CHAPTER 2
CROP BY CROP

On the following twenty-seven pages are listed the most popular vegetables grown in British gardens. The printed text tells you what to do and when to do it. You can then write down in the spaces provided what you actually did, and so build up a permanent record and a useful reminder for next season.

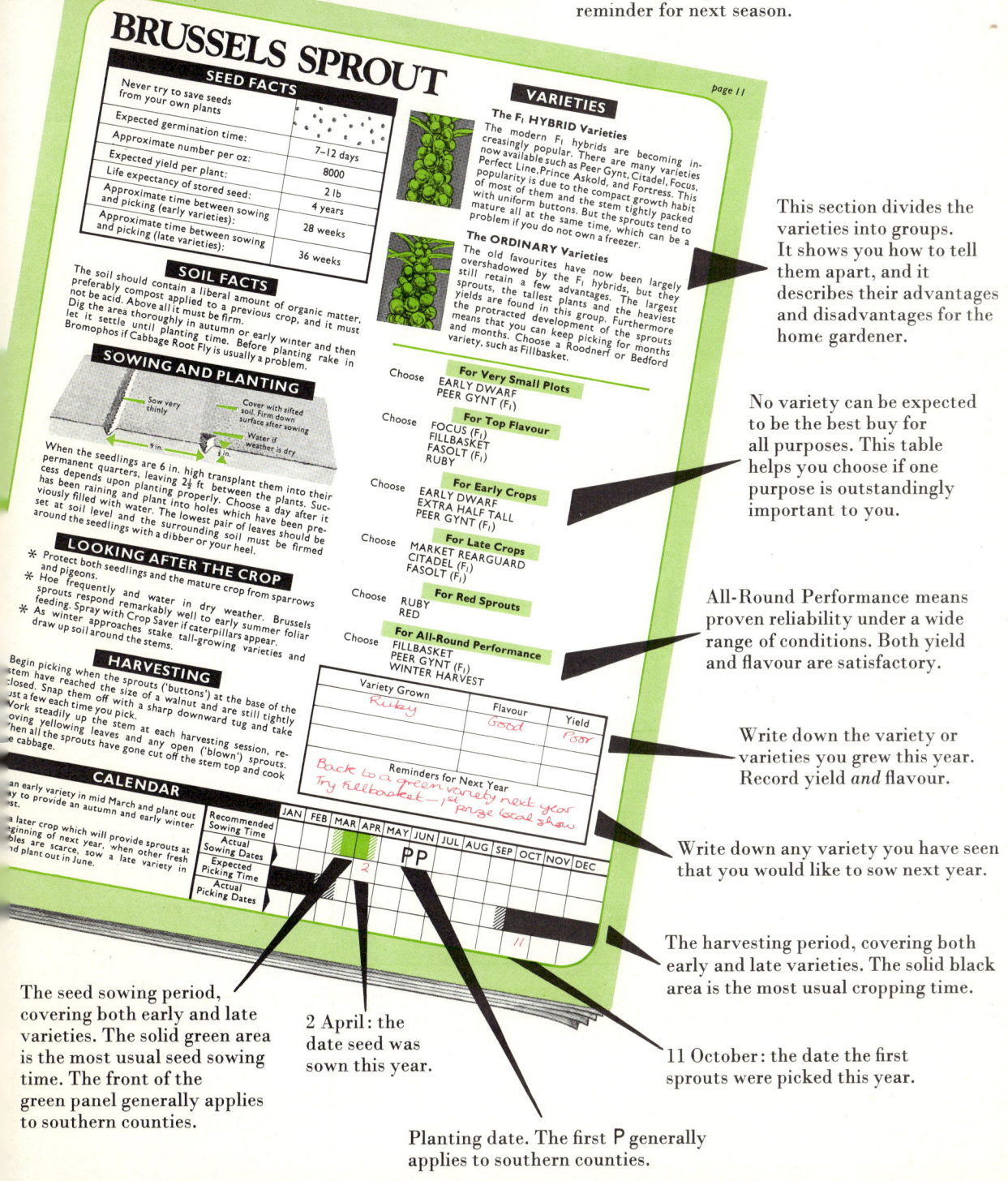

BRUSSELS SPROUT

SEED FACTS

Never try to save seeds from your own plants

Expected germination time:	7–12 days
Approximate number per oz:	8000
Expected yield per plant:	2 lb
Life expectancy of stored seed:	4 years
Approximate time between sowing and picking (early varieties):	28 weeks
Approximate time between sowing and picking (late varieties):	36 weeks

SOIL FACTS

The soil should contain a liberal amount of organic matter, preferably compost applied to a previous crop, and it must not be acid. Above all it must be firm. Dig the area thoroughly in autumn or early winter and then let it settle until planting time. Before planting rake in Bromophos if Cabbage Root Fly is usually a problem.

SOWING AND PLANTING

Sow very thinly. Cover with sifted soil. Firm down surface after sowing. Water if weather is dry. 9 in. / ½ in.

When the seedlings are 6 in. high transplant them into their permanent quarters, leaving 2½ ft between the plants. Success depends upon planting properly. Choose a day after it has been raining and plant into holes which have been previously filled with water. The lowest pair of leaves should be set at soil level and the surrounding soil must be firmed around the seedlings with a dibber or your heel.

LOOKING AFTER THE CROP

* Protect both seedlings and the mature crop from sparrows and pigeons.
* Hoe frequently and water in dry weather. Brussels sprouts respond remarkably well to early summer foliar feeding. Spray with Crop Saver if caterpillars appear.
* As winter approaches stake tall-growing varieties and draw up soil around the stems.

HARVESTING

Begin picking when the sprouts ('buttons') at the base of the stem have reached the size of a walnut and are still tightly closed. Snap them off with a sharp downward tug and take just a few each time you pick. Work steadily up the stem at each harvesting session, removing yellowing leaves and any open ('blown') sprouts. When all the sprouts have gone cut off the stem top and cook like cabbage.

CALENDAR

An early variety in mid March and plant out [...] to provide an autumn and early winter [...].

A later crop which will provide sprouts at [beginning] of next year, when other fresh [vegetab]les are scarce, sow a late variety in [...] and plant out in June.

VARIETIES

The F₁ HYBRID Varieties
The modern F₁ hybrids are becoming increasingly popular. There are many varieties now available such as Peer Gynt, Citadel, Focus, Perfect Line, Prince Askold, and Fortress. This popularity is due to the compact growth habit of most of them and the stem tightly packed with uniform buttons. But the sprouts tend to mature all at the same time, which can be a problem if you do not own a freezer.

The ORDINARY Varieties
The old favourites have now been largely overshadowed by the F₁ hybrids, but they still retain a few advantages. The largest sprouts, the tallest plants and the heaviest yields are found in this group. Furthermore the protracted development of the sprouts means that you can keep picking for months and months. Choose a Roodnerf or Bedford variety, such as Fillbasket.

Choose	For Very Small Plots
	EARLY DWARF PEER GYNT (F₁)
Choose	**For Top Flavour**
	FOCUS (F₁) FILLBASKET FASOLT (F₁) RUBY
Choose	**For Early Crops**
	EARLY DWARF EXTRA HALF TALL PEER GYNT (F₁)
Choose	**For Late Crops**
	MARKET REARGUARD CITADEL (F₁) FASOLT (F₁)
Choose	**For Red Sprouts**
	RUBY RED
Choose	**For All-Round Performance**
	FILLBASKET PEER GYNT (F₁) WINTER HARVEST

Variety Grown	Flavour	Yield
Ruby	Good	Poor

Reminders for Next Year
Back to a green variety next year
Try Fillbasket — 1st prize local show

	JAN	FEB	MAR	APR	MAY	JUN	JUL	AUG	SEP	OCT	NOV	DEC
Recommended Sowing Time			■									
Actual Sowing Dates				2								
Expected Picking Time					P	P						
Actual Picking Dates										11		

This section divides the varieties into groups. It shows you how to tell them apart, and it describes their advantages and disadvantages for the home gardener.

No variety can be expected to be the best buy for all purposes. This table helps you choose if one purpose is outstandingly important to you.

All-Round Performance means proven reliability under a wide range of conditions. Both yield and flavour are satisfactory.

Write down the variety or varieties you grew this year. Record yield *and* flavour.

Write down any variety you have seen that you would like to sow next year.

The harvesting period, covering both early and late varieties. The solid black area is the most usual cropping time.

The seed sowing period, covering both early and late varieties. The solid green area is the most usual seed sowing time. The front of the green panel generally applies to southern counties.

2 April: the date seed was sown this year.

11 October: the date the first sprouts were picked this year.

Planting date. The first P generally applies to southern counties.

BROAD BEAN

SEED FACTS

Types available:	Green bean varieties / White bean varieties
Points to watch for:	Discard all seed which has small, round holes
Expected germination time:	10-14 days
Approximate number per pint:	200
Amount to buy for a 15 ft double row:	¼ pint
Expected yield from a 15 ft double row:	16 lb
Life expectancy of stored seed:	2 years
Approximate time between autumn sowing and picking:	28 weeks
Approximate time between spring sowing and picking:	16 weeks

SOIL FACTS

Nearly every soil will produce an adequate crop, provided it is neither very acid nor waterlogged. Apply a balanced fertilizer, such as Growmore or Crop Booster, about 1 week before sowing. Lime if necessary.

The ideal soil is rich and free-draining. Manure or compost will have been applied for the previous crop.

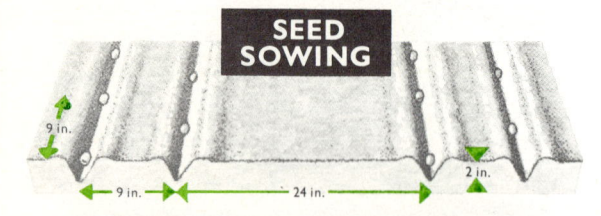

SEED SOWING

(9 in. deep; 9 in. apart; 24 in. between rows; 2 in. apart)

LOOKING AFTER THE CROP

* Hoe regularly and keep the plants watered in dry weather.
* Pinch off the top 3 in. of stem as soon as the first beans start to form. This will ensure an earlier harvest and also provide some degree of blackfly control. This serious pest *must* be kept down, so spray with Crop Saver or Topgard if attacks persist.
* Support tall-growing varieties with canes and string.

HARVESTING

Do not let the pods reach their maximum size unless you are exhibiting or saving seed. Pick when the pods are plump but while the scar on each shelled bean is still white or green. (scar not black)
Broad beans are excellent for home freezing. Baby pods (2 in. long) can be cooked whole like french beans.

VARIETIES

The LONGPOD Varieties
Recognised by their long, narrow pods. This is the best group for hardiness, early cropping, exhibiting and top yields.

The WINDSOR Varieties
Recognised by their shorter, broader pods. This is the best group for flavour. They are not suitable for autumn planting, and they mature later than the Longpods.

The DWARF Varieties
Recognised by their short pods and dwarf, bushy growth habit. They should be grown as a single row. This is the best group for small or exposed plots.

For Top Flavour
Choose RED EPICURE (unique reddish-brown beans)
Also recommended are the WINDSOR varieties.

For Top Yields
Choose IMPERIAL LONGPOD
EXHIBITION LONGPOD — 14 in. pods, containing 8-9 beans.
COLOSSAL
LONGFELLOW

For Autumn Sowing
Choose AQUADULCE
BUNYARD'S EXHIBITION

For Early Crops
Choose MAJOR for spring sowing

For Very Small Plots
Choose THE SUTTON
THE MIDGET

For All-Round Performance
Choose BUNYARD'S EXHIBITION
MASTERPIECE

Variety Grown	Flavour	Yield

Reminders for Next Year

CALENDAR

November sowing will provide beans in early June, but there can be heavy losses in a severe winter. Only attempt autumn sowing if your plot is sheltered, free draining and located in a mild area. It is generally much more satisfactory to sow an early variety in March or plant out greenhouse-raised seedlings in April if you want an early summer harvest.

	JAN	FEB	MAR	APR	MAY	JUN	JUL	AUG	SEP	OCT	NOV	DEC
Recommended Sowing Time		■	■	■	▨						▨	
Actual Sowing Dates												
Expected Picking Time						▨	■	▨	▨			
Actual Picking Dates												

FRENCH BEAN

SEED FACTS

Seed will rot if planted in cold soil	
Expected germination time:	14-20 days
Approximate number per pint:	1000
Amount to buy for a 30 ft row:	$\frac{1}{8}$ pint
Expected yield from a 30 ft row (Dwarf variety):	20 lb
Expected yield from a 30 ft row (Climbing variety):	30 lb
Expected yield from a 30 ft row (as dried beans):	2 lb
Life expectancy of stored seed:	2 years
Approximate time between sowing and picking:	10-13 weeks

SOIL FACTS

French beans will succeed in any soil provided it is neither very heavy nor acid. For really good results the soil should be well dug and should contain well-rotted compost or manure. Before sowing apply fertilizer and rake to produce a fine tilth.

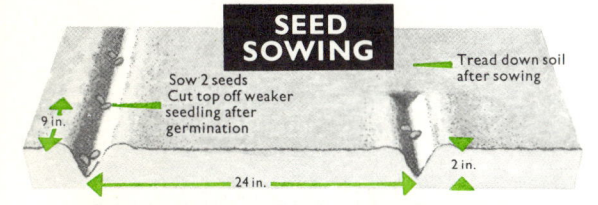

SEED SOWING

Sow 2 seeds Cut top off weaker seedling after germination
Tread down soil after sowing
9 in. 24 in. 2 in.

LOOKING AFTER THE CROP

* Protect seedlings from slugs. Hoe regularly and water during dry weather.
* Support the plants with short twigs or pea sticks to prevent them toppling over. Use twiggy branches or plastic netting for climbing varieties.
* When flowers appear spray regularly with water to help pod formation. Add Fillip to prolong cropping.

HARVESTING

Begin picking when the pods are about 4 in. long. A pod is ready when it snaps easily when bent and before the tell-tale bulges of maturity appear along its length. Pick several times a week to prevent any pods maturing; you can then expect to continue cropping for 5-8 weeks. Take care not to loosen the plant when harvesting.
French beans are excellent for home freezing; choose a stringless variety. Dried beans (Haricots) are obtained by leaving the pods on the plant until they turn straw-coloured. Then hang up the plants indoors to dry. When the pods are brittle shell the beans and dry them on a sheet of paper for several days. Store the haricot beans in a closed container.

VARIETIES

Most french beans are dwarfs, growing only 12 in. high. Climbing french beans are available, their 5 ft stems requiring support.

The GREEN Varieties

Flat-podded   Pencil-podded

These make up the most popular group, with scores of old and new favourites. The well-established varieties, such as Canadian Wonder and The Prince, are flat-podded and can be stringy when mature. Many of the new introductions are pencil-podded and entirely stringless.

The COLOURED Varieties

Yellow   Purple

Coloured pods have an obvious novelty value, but they do have other advantages. The pods can be easily seen at picking time and the stringless yellow beans (Waxpods) have an excellent flavour.

For Top Flavour
Choose   KINGHORN WAXPOD
         ROYALTY
         ROMANO (Climbing variety)

For Top Yields
Choose   MASTERPIECE
         BREZO
         THE PRINCE

For Early Crops
Choose   LIMELIGHT
         EARLIGREEN
         TENDERGREEN

For Poor Growing Conditions
Choose   GLAMIS
         CANADIAN WONDER
         ROYALTY

For Continental-Style Beans
Choose   REMUS
         SPRITE
         LOCH NESS

For Exhibiting and All-Round Performance
Choose   THE PRINCE
         MASTERPIECE

Variety Grown	Flavour	Yield
Reminders for Next Year		

CALENDAR

For an early crop sow a quick-maturing variety at the beginning of May. Under cloches you can begin a month earlier and pick beans in June.
The maincrop is sown during May and early June. Successional sowings will provide pods until early October.
For a late autumn crop sow in July and cover the plants with cloches in October.

	JAN	FEB	MAR	APR	MAY	JUN	JUL	AUG	SEP	OCT	NOV	DEC
Recommended Sowing Time				▨	▇	▇	▨					
Actual Sowing Dates												
Expected Picking Time							▨	▇	▇	▨		
Actual Picking Dates												

RUNNER BEAN

SEED FACTS

Do not soak seed before planting	
Expected germination time:	10-14 days
Approximate number per pint:	300
Amount to buy for a 15 ft double row:	¼ pint
Expected yield from a 15 ft double row:	100 lb
Life expectancy of stored seed:	2 years
Approximate time between sowing and picking:	12-14 weeks

SOIL FACTS

Pick a sheltered spot and prepare the soil in winter or early spring. Dig a trench about 18 in. wide and fork in a liberal amount of compost or manure before replacing the soil. Rake in a general fertilizer such as Crop Booster shortly before sowing.

Runner beans will not succeed in heavy clays, shallow sands nor in very cold areas.

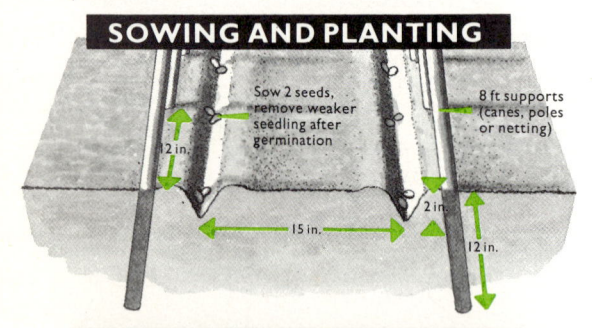

SOWING AND PLANTING

Sow 2 seeds, remove weaker seedling after germination. 8 ft supports (canes, poles or netting). 12 in., 15 in., 2 in., 12 in.

LOOKING AFTER THE CROP

* Loosely tie the young plants to the supports, after which they will climb naturally. Protect from slugs.
* Hoe regularly and water copiously if the weather is dry. Liquid feed with Bio or Fillip during July and August. Mulching will help to conserve moisture.
* Remove the growing points when the plants reach the tops of the supports. Spray the plants regularly with water to help pod formation.

HARVESTING

Pick regularly once the pods have reached a decent size but before the beans inside have started to swell. If you remove all the pods as soon as they reach this stage then harvesting should continue for about 8 weeks. But if you allow even a small number of pods to ripen then further production will cease.

If there is a glut then the excess can be frozen, salted or dried as haricot beans.

VARIETIES

Most varieties are 'Scarlet Runners' with attractive red flowers and green pods. Other colours are available.

STICK Runner Beans

Nearly all runner beans are bred to grow 8-10 ft high and bear pods which are 10-20 in. long. They are grown on tall supports.

GROUND Runner Beans

A few varieties (Kelvedon Marvel, Kelvedon Wonder and Sunset) which are naturally tall-growing are sometimes sown 2 ft apart and grown as short, bushy and early-cropping plants by pinching out the main stem when the plants are about 12 in. high. Side shoots are pinched out at weekly intervals and the stems should be supported with short twigs. Pods tend to grow curved and twisted.

DWARF Runner Beans

Two true dwarfs (Hammond's Dwarf White and Hammond's Dwarf Scarlet) are available. Plants grow about 18 in. high and the pods are 8 in. long.

For Top Flavour
Choose ENORMA
FRY

For Top Yields
Choose PRIZEWINNER
GOLIATH
AS LONG AS YOUR ARM

For Early Crops
Choose HAMMOND'S DWARF SCARLET
KELVEDON MARVEL
SUNSET (pale pink flowers)
SCARLET EMPEROR

For Prize-Winning Pods
Choose ENORMA
YARDSTICK
CRUSADER

For All-Round Performance
Choose CRUSADER
SCARLET EMPEROR
YARDSTICK
STREAMLINE

Variety Grown	Flavour	Yield
Reminders for Next Year		

CALENDAR

The standard method of raising runner beans is to sow the seeds outdoors at the end of May, with a second sowing in June for a late crop in mild areas. Alternatively, seedlings can be raised under glass by sowing in early May and then planting out at the beginning of June. This method is strongly recommended for the colder areas of the country.

	JAN	FEB	MAR	APR	MAY	JUN	JUL	AUG	SEP	OCT	NOV	DEC
Recommended Sowing Time						P						
Actual Sowing Dates												
Expected Picking Time												
Actual Picking Dates												

BEETROOT

SEED FACTS

'Seed' is really a cluster, each one containing several true seeds	
Pelleted seed is available.	
Expected germination time (Soak seed overnight before sowing to hasten germination):	12-21 days
Amount to buy for a 30 ft row:	¼ oz
Expected yield from a 30 ft row (maincrop):	27 lb
Life expectancy of stored seed:	2 years
Approximate time between sowing and picking (early):	9 weeks
Approximate time between sowing and picking (maincrop):	16 weeks

SOIL FACTS

Beetroot will not succeed in raw clay, and the soil must contain enough organic matter to prevent rapid drying out during the summer months.

Most garden soils will produce a good crop provided you do not add fresh organic matter when preparing the ground. Peat or well-rotted compost is suitable. Trace elements are necessary so apply Crop Booster, which contains seaweed, shortly before sowing.

SEED SOWING

(4 in. deep drills, 2 or 3 'seeds', 12 in. apart, 1 in.)

LOOKING AFTER THE CROP

* Thin out the seedlings so that just one plant remains at each position. Protection against birds may be necessary.
* Hoe regularly but *never* touch the roots or they will be ruined. Dryness at the root can lead to coarse texture or bolting; the sudden return to moist conditions can lead to splitting. So regular watering during dry weather is essential, and mulching will help to conserve moisture.
* Pull out alternate plants to provide young tender roots for immediate use. The remainder can be allowed to mature as a maincrop for late use or storage.

HARVESTING

Pull small beetroots as required. The maincrop grown for storage should be *carefully* lifted by hand in early October.

Discard all damaged roots. Shake off soil and twist off tops, leaving about 2 in. of stem. Place the roots between layers of dry peat or sand in a stout box and store in a shed. The crop will keep until March.

VARIETIES

The GLOBE Varieties (G)

By far the most popular beetroot group for the amateur, as they are a convenient size for kitchen use. Both early and maincrop varieties are available. Yellow, white and bolt-resistant types have been recently introduced.

The TANKARD Varieties (T)

Very few varieties of this group are available, the most widely grown being Cylindra, Housewives' Choice and Feltham Intermediate. Sometimes described as 'Intermediate' or 'Cylindrical', these beetroots are grown for winter storage.

The LONG Varieties (L)

Long beetroots need deep sandy loam in the garden and a very large pan in the kitchen, so they are not really suitable for the ordinary garden plot. They are the beetroots for the keen exhibitor.

For Top Flavour
Choose the new taste –
- GOLDEN (G)
- SNOWHITE (G)

or a sweet red –
- CRIMSON GLOBE (G)
- DETROIT GLOBE (G)

For Early Sowing
Choose
- AVONEARLY (G)
- BOLTARDY (G)
- EARLY BUNCH (G)

For Storage
Choose
- DETROIT GLOBE (G)
- CYLINDRA (T)

For Exhibiting
Choose
- SUTTONS GLOBE (G)
- LONG BLOOD RED (L)

For All-Round Performance
Choose
- CRIMSON GLOBE (G)
- DETROIT GLOBE (G)

Variety Grown	Flavour	Yield
Reminders for Next Year		

CALENDAR

For a very early crop sow a bolt-resistant variety under cloches in March.

The main sowing time begins outdoors in late April and successional sowings will provide a regular supply of tender roots. When growing for winter storage sow in June. The roots from earlier sowings may be too coarse at lifting time in early October.

For a late autumn crop sow Little Ball in July.

	JAN	FEB	MAR	APR	MAY	JUN	JUL	AUG	SEP	OCT	NOV	DEC
Recommended Sowing Time			▨	▨	▩	▩						
Actual Sowing Dates												
Expected Picking Time						▨	▩	▩	▩	▩	▨	▨
Actual Picking Dates												

SPROUTING BROCCOLI

SEED FACTS

F_1 hybrid seed is available (see page 4)	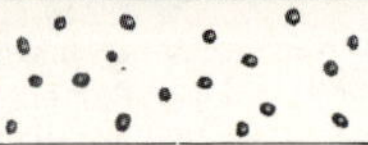
Expected germination time:	7-12 days
Approximate number per oz:	8000
Expected yield per plant:	1½ lb
Life expectancy of stored seed:	3 years
Approximate time between sowing and picking (Green varieties):	12 weeks
Approximate time between sowing and picking (Purple and White varieties):	40 weeks

SOIL FACTS

Sprouting broccoli, like other brassicas, can fail in loose and starved soil. Ideally the ground should be rather heavy, rich in organic matter, and *firm*. A rather sheltered spot is best. Rake in Bromophos if Cabbage Root Fly is usually a problem.

SOWING AND PLANTING

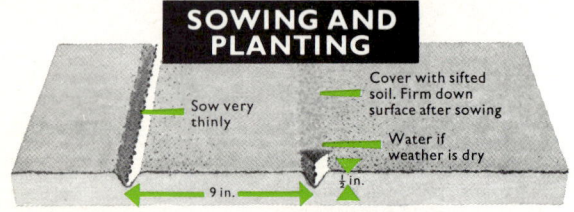

Sow very thinly. Cover with sifted soil. Firm down surface after sowing. Water if weather is dry. 9 in. ½ in.

If the seedlings are overcrowded then thin as soon as possible to prevent the plants becoming weak and spindly. When the seedlings are 3 in. high transplant them into their permanent quarters, leaving 2 ft between the plants.
Plant firmly and set them about 1 in. deeper than they were growing in the seedbed. Water well in.

LOOKING AFTER THE CROP

* Hoe regularly and provide some protection against birds.
* Summer care consists of watering in dry weather and applying a mulch to conserve moisture. Occasional feeding will improve the crop. Spray with Crop Saver if caterpillars appear.
* With the approach of winter draw up soil around the stems and stake if the site is exposed. Always firm the plants if they are loosened by wind or frost.

HARVESTING

The time to cut is when the flower shoots ('spears') are well formed but before the small flower buds have opened.
Cut the central spear first; in some varieties this will be quite a large cauliflower-like head. Then cut the side spears, which should be about 4 in. long, as they develop. Never let them flower or production will stop. Broccoli spears are suitable for deep freezing.

VARIETIES

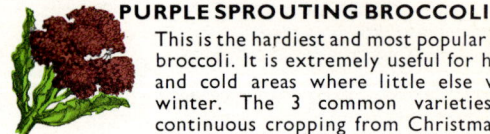

PURPLE SPROUTING BROCCOLI
This is the hardiest and most popular sprouting broccoli. It is extremely useful for heavy soils and cold areas where little else will over-winter. The 3 common varieties provide continuous cropping from Christmas to May.

Choose CHRISTMAS PURPLE SPROUTING (Jan-Feb)
EARLY PURPLE SPROUTING (Feb-Mar)
LATE PURPLE SPROUTING (April-May)

WHITE SPROUTING BROCCOLI
This group produces small cauliflower-like spears which some people consider to have a finer flavour and better appearance than the more popular purple varieties.

Choose EARLY WHITE SPROUTING (Mar-April)
LATE WHITE SPROUTING (April-May)

GREEN SPROUTING BROCCOLI
Green sprouting broccoli, or Calabrese, is an underrated but extremely useful vegetable, as it produces delicately-flavoured spears from August to the end of October.

For One Large Head
Choose GREEN COMET (F_1)

For Green Broccoli Spears
Choose EXPRESS CORONA (F_1) – Early
ITALIAN SPROUTING – Top Flavour
AUTUMN SPEAR – Late
EL CENTRO

PERENNIAL BROCCOLI
This tall-growing perennial will yield about 8 small, pale green heads in spring or early summer year after year. Plant against a fence and mulch annually.

Choose NINE-STAR PERENNIAL

Variety Grown	Flavour	Yield
Reminders for Next Year		

CALENDAR

The date you can expect to start harvesting depends upon the variety and the weather. Early Purple Sprouting will be ready for its first picking in January in a mild winter, and the less hardy Green Sprouting Broccoli will go on cropping throughout the winter if prolonged frosts do not occur.

	JAN	FEB	MAR	APR	MAY	JUN	JUL	AUG	SEP	OCT	NOV	DEC
Recommended Sowing Time				■	P	P	P					
Actual Sowing Dates												
Expected Picking Time	EARLY vars.	EARLY vars.	LATE vars.	LATE vars.				GREEN vars.	GREEN vars.	GREEN vars.		
Actual Picking Dates												

BRUSSELS SPROUT

SEED FACTS

Never try to save seeds from your own plants	
Expected germination time:	7–12 days
Approximate number per oz:	8000
Expected yield per plant:	2 lb
Life expectancy of stored seed:	4 years
Approximate time between sowing and picking (early varieties):	28 weeks
Approximate time between sowing and picking (late varieties):	36 weeks

SOIL FACTS

The soil should contain a liberal amount of organic matter, preferably compost applied to a previous crop, and it must not be acid. Above all it must be firm.

Dig the area thoroughly in autumn or early winter and then let it settle until planting time. Before planting rake in Bromophos if Cabbage Root Fly is usually a problem.

SOWING AND PLANTING

Sow very thinly. Cover with sifted soil. Firm down surface after sowing. Water if weather is dry. 9 in. ½ in.

When the seedlings are 6 in. high transplant them into their permanent quarters, leaving 2½ ft between the plants. Success depends upon planting properly. Choose a day after it has been raining and plant into holes which have been previously filled with water. The lowest pair of leaves should be set at soil level and the surrounding soil must be firmed around the seedlings with a dibber or your heel.

LOOKING AFTER THE CROP

* Protect both seedlings and the mature crop from sparrows and pigeons.
* Hoe frequently and water in dry weather. Brussels sprouts respond remarkably well to early summer foliar feeding. Spray with Crop Saver if caterpillars appear.
* As winter approaches stake tall-growing varieties and draw up soil around the stems.

HARVESTING

Begin picking when the sprouts ('buttons') at the base of the stem have reached the size of a walnut and are still tightly closed. Snap them off with a sharp downward tug and take just a few each time you pick.

Work steadily up the stem at each harvesting session, removing yellowing leaves and any open ('blown') sprouts. When all the sprouts have gone cut off the stem top and cook like cabbage.

VARIETIES

The F_1 HYBRID Varieties

The modern F_1 hybrids are becoming increasingly popular. There are many varieties now available such as Peer Gynt, Citadel, Focus, Perfect Line, Prince Askold, and Fortress. This popularity is due to the compact growth habit of most of them and the stem tightly packed with uniform buttons. But the sprouts tend to mature all at the same time, which can be a problem if you do not own a freezer.

The ORDINARY Varieties

The old favourites have now been largely overshadowed by the F_1 hybrids, but they still retain a few advantages. The largest sprouts, the tallest plants and the heaviest yields are found in this group. Furthermore the protracted development of the sprouts means that you can keep picking for months and months. Choose a Roodnerf or Bedford variety, such as Fillbasket.

For Very Small Plots
Choose EARLY DWARF
PEER GYNT (F_1)

For Top Flavour
Choose FOCUS (F_1)
FILLBASKET
FASOLT (F_1)
RUBY

For Early Crops
Choose EARLY DWARF
EXTRA HALF TALL
PEER GYNT (F_1)

For Late Crops
Choose MARKET REARGUARD
CITADEL (F_1)
FASOLT (F_1)

For Red Sprouts
Choose RUBY
RED

For All-Round Performance
Choose FILLBASKET
PEER GYNT (F_1)
WINTER HARVEST

Variety Grown	Flavour	Yield

Reminders for Next Year

CALENDAR

Sow an early variety in mid March and plant out in May to provide an autumn and early winter harvest.

For a later crop which will provide sprouts at the beginning of next year, when other fresh vegetables are scarce, sow a late variety in April and plant out in June.

	JAN	FEB	MAR	APR	MAY	JUN	JUL	AUG	SEP	OCT	NOV	DEC
Recommended Sowing Time			▨	▨	P	P						
Actual Sowing Dates												
Expected Picking Time			▨						▨			
Actual Picking Dates												

CABBAGE

SEED FACTS

Don't sow too many at one time – just a very small row every few weeks	
Expected germination time:	7–12 days
Approximate number per oz:	7000
Expected yield per plant:	1–3 lb
Life expectancy of stored seed:	3 years
Approximate time between sowing and harvesting (Spring varieties):	35 weeks
Approximate time between sowing and harvesting (Summer & Winter varieties):	20–35 weeks

SOIL FACTS

All cabbage varieties require well-consolidated soil, so the basic requirement is to leave several months between digging and planting. Add organic matter when digging. If you cannot afford land to stand idle then plant into an area recently vacated by an unrelated crop. Lime if necessary.

Just before planting rake in the standard soil trouble preventatives (see page 14). Apply a general fertilizer for all types except Spring cabbage as this group needs to be grown slowly in a sheltered spot.

SOWING AND PLANTING

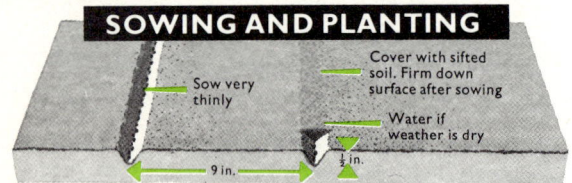

Sow very thinly. Cover with sifted soil. Firm down surface after sowing. Water if weather is dry. 9 in. ½ in.

Lift and transplant the seedlings when the soil is moist. The stems should have 5–6 leaves and remember to plant *firmly*. Water thoroughly after planting. Allow 1½ ft between the plants if the variety is compact; leave 2 ft either way if the variety is large. With Spring cabbage leave only 6 in. between plants in rows 1½ ft apart; the thinnings will provide "spring greens" in March.

LOOKING AFTER THE CROP

* Hoe carefully until the crop is large enough to suppress weeds. Spray with Crop Saver at the first sign of caterpillars, Flea Beetle or White Fly.
* Water if the weather is dry. Liquid feed as the heads approach maturity.
* During winter firm down any plants which have been loosened by wind or frost.

HARVESTING

In February and March thin out the Spring cabbage rows and use the young plants as "spring greens". Leave remaining plants 1½ ft apart to mature in April–June. Cut Summer and Winter varieties as required.

VARIETIES

The SPRING Varieties (Sp)
These cabbages are planted in the autumn to provide tender "spring greens" in early spring and mature heads later in the season. They are generally conical in shape, and smaller than the Summer and Winter varieties. Examples are Early Market, Harbinger, April, Flower of Spring and Wheelers' Imperial.

The SUMMER Varieties (Su)
These cabbages mature in midsummer. They are generally ball-shaped, with a few exceptions such as the ever-popular Greyhound and the new F_1 hybrid Hispi which are conical. Examples of the reliable Summer cabbages are Golden Acre, May Star, Stonehead, Primo, Green Express and Velocity. Red varieties include Niggerhead, Ruby Ball and Large Blood Red.

The WINTER Varieties (W)
These cabbages mature in autumn, winter or early spring. The quicker-maturing types, such as Winnigstadt, Autumn Supreme and Wiam are ready between August and November. The later types, such as January King and Christmas Drumhead, mature between November and February. Included in this group are the Savoy cabbages (Savoy King, Ice Queen, Best of All, Rearguard etc.) which are easily recognizable by their crisp and puckered dark-green leaves.

Choose — **For Very Small Plots**
- EARLIEST (Su)
- WHEELERS' IMPERIAL (Sp)
- DURHAM ELF (Sp)

Choose — **For Top Flavour**
- DURHAM EARLY (Sp)
- GREEN EXPRESS (Su)
- HISPI (Su)

Choose — **For All-Round Performance**
- WHEELERS' IMPERIAL (Sp)
- GREYHOUND (Su)
- WINNIGSTADT (W)
- JANUARY KING (W)

Variety Grown	Flavour	Yield
Durham Early		

Reminders for Next Year

CALENDAR

Spring varieties: Sow in July – August and transplant in September–October.

Summer varieties: Sow outdoors in April and transplant in May or early June for an August crop. For June cabbage sow under glass in February and plant out in early April.

Winter varieties: Sow outdoors at the end of April or in May and transplant during June.

	JAN	FEB	MAR	APR	MAY	JUN	JUL	AUG	SEP	OCT	NOV	DEC
Recommended Sowing Time				P	P	P			P	P		
Actual Sowing Dates												
Expected Picking Time	WINTER VARS.		SPRING VARS.				SUMMER VARS.			WINTER VARS.		
Actual Picking Dates												

CARROT

SEED FACTS

Seed is small. Mix with dry peat before sowing	
Pelleted seed is available	
Expected germination time:	14 days
Amount to buy for a 30 ft row:	¼ oz
Expected yield from a 30 ft row (maincrop):	25 lb
Life expectancy of stored seed:	4 years
Approximate time between sowing and picking (early):	14 weeks
Approximate time between sowing and picking (maincrop):	16 weeks

SOIL FACTS

Carrots are hard to please. The soil must be deep, rich and rather sandy if you want to grow fine specimens. Many soils will produce satisfactory crops, but clays and soils containing fresh compost or manure should not be used for carrots. Before sowing rake in Bromophos to prevent carrot fly and wireworm attacks.

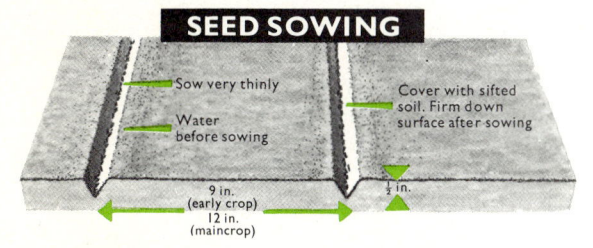

SEED SOWING

- Sow very thinly
- Water before sowing
- Cover with sifted soil. Firm down surface after sowing
- 9 in. (early crop)
- 12 in. (maincrop)
- ½ in.

LOOKING AFTER THE CROP

* Thin out the crop as soon as the seedlings are large enough to handle. Then thin once or twice more until the plants are 3-6 in. apart. The final thinnings will provide small, tender roots for the kitchen.
* Take care when thinning or the root-ruining carrot fly will be attracted to your garden. Water if the soil is dry and then thin in the evening. Finally firm the soil around the remaining plants and burn or bury the thinnings.
* Keep the soil hoed and remember to water in dry weather. Rain following a dry spell is the cause of root splitting.

HARVESTING

Pull small carrots as required. Lift the maincrop grown for storage during October. Remove soil from carrots to be stored and cut off leaves to about ½ in. above the crowns. Place them between layers of dry peat or sand in a stout box. Store in a shed and the crop will keep until March.

VARIETIES

The SHORT-ROOTED Varieties (S)

Golf ball round or finger long, these short-rooted carrots mature quickly. They are the first to be sown, and the early crop is either used immediately or frozen. They are renowned for their flavour.

The INTERMEDIATE-ROOTED Varieties (I)

These medium-sized carrots are the best all-rounders for the average garden. They are sown later than the Short varieties, the young roots being pulled for immediate use and the remainder allowed to mature as a maincrop for winter storage.

The LONG-ROOTED Varieties (L)

These are the long, tapered giants of the show bench. They are usually grown in specially prepared soil and are not for general garden use unless your ground is deep, rich and free-draining.

For Top Flavour
Choose AMSTERDAM FORCING (S)
EARLY NANTES (S)
SWEETHEART (S)
SHORT 'N' SWEET (S)

For Heavy, Shallow or Stony Soil
Choose PARIS FORCING (S)
PARISIAN RONDO (S)

For Top Yields and Storage
Choose AUTUMN KING (I)
SCARLET PERFECTION (I)

For Exhibiting
Choose ST. VALERY (L)
NEW RED INTERMEDIATE (L)

For All-Round Performance
Choose CHANTENEY RED CORED (I)
JAMES SCARLET INTERMEDIATE (I)
NANTES TIP TOP (I)
FAVOURITE (I)

Variety Grown	Flavour	Yield

Reminders for Next Year

CALENDAR

	JAN	FEB	MAR	APR	MAY	JUN	JUL	AUG	SEP	OCT	NOV	DEC
Recommended Sowing Time			■	■	■	■		▨				
Actual Sowing Dates												
Expected Picking Time						■	■	■	■	■	▨	
Actual Picking Dates												

Sow short-rooted varieties from March onwards for an early crop.

Sow other varieties between mid April and early July for picking as maincrops in October.

For a tender crop of carrots in November and December, sow a short-rooted variety in August and cover with cloches in October.

CAULIFLOWER

SEED FACTS

Pelleted seed is available	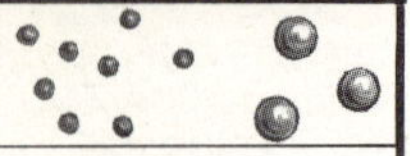
Expected germination time:	7–12 days
Approximate number per oz:	8000
Expected yield per plant:	1–2 lb
Life expectancy of stored seed:	3 years
Approximate time between sowing and picking (Summer/Autumn varieties):	18–24 weeks
Approximate time between sowing and picking (Winter varieties):	40 weeks

SOIL FACTS

Thorough soil preparation is one of the secrets of successful cauliflower growing. Dig the soil in autumn or early winter and incorporate as much organic matter as you can. Lime if necessary. Let the ground settle until just before planting time. Then rake in a general fertilizer, and also apply Bromophos for Cabbage Root Fly and Calomel Dust for Club Root control if these troubles are prevalent in your area.

SOWING AND PLANTING

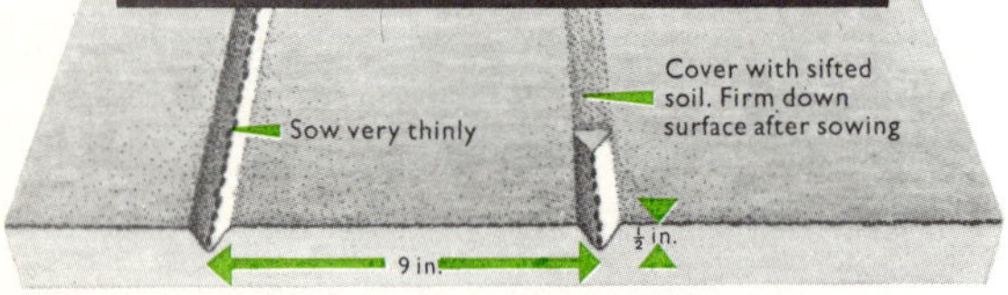

Cover with sifted soil. Firm down surface after sowing
Sow very thinly
9 in
½ in.

Lift seedlings carefully with as much soil as possible around the roots when the small plants have about 6 leaves. Choose a day when the soil contains plenty of moisture and set the plants about 2 ft apart. Don't bury them deeply – keep to the same level as in the seedbed. Plant firmly and water in to aid rapid establishment.

LOOKING AFTER THE CROP

* Cauliflowers must never be kept short of water, especially in the early stages, or very small heads will quickly form.
* Feed occasionally as cauliflowers are a hungry crop. With Summer varieties bend a few leaves over the developing curd to protect it from the sun.
* Protect the Winter crop from snow and frost by breaking a few leaves over the curd.

HARVESTING

Begin cutting cauliflowers while they are still fairly small rather than waiting for them to mature all at once. In this way you can prolong the harvesting period. Cut in the morning when the heads still have dew on them, but in frosty weather wait until midday. If you wish to keep the heads for a week or two before use lift the plants and hang them upside down in a cool shed.

VARIETIES

The SUMMER Varieties (S)
These cauliflowers mature during the summer months from seed sown in a cold frame in September, heated glass in January or outdoors in April. They are compact plants, and you can choose a very early variety, such as Classic, Delta, Snow King, Polaris and Snowball or a rather late-maturing variety such as All the Year Round or Le Cerf.

The AUTUMN Varieties (A)
These cauliflowers mature during the autumn months and are of two distinctly different types. There are the large and vigorous varieties such as Veitch's Autumn Giant, Beacon, and Majestic. There are also the dwarf Australian varieties such as Barrier Reef, Kangaroo and Canberra.

The WINTER Varieties (W)
These 'cauliflowers' are Heading Broccoli (note incurving leaves) and although less delicately-flavoured than true cauliflowers they are easier to grow. They mature between winter and early summer depending upon the variety. Choose an Extra-Hardy type such as Thanet, St. George and Reading Giant.

For Small Gardens
Choose EARLY SNOWBALL (S)
  ARCTURUS (S)
  BONDI (A)
  LATE QUEEN (W)

For Large Heads
Choose POLARIS (S)
  WHITE HEART (A)
  ST. GEORGE (W)

For Exhibiting
Choose DOMINANT (S)
  KANGAROO (A)
  BEACON (A)

For All-Round Performance
Choose ALL THE YEAR ROUND (S)
  VEITCH'S AUTUMN GIANT (A)
  ST. GEORGE (W)

Variety Grown	Flavour	Yield

Reminders for Next Year

CALENDAR

Summer varieties: In April transplant seedlings which have been raised under glass from a January sowing to provide a June-July crop. Or sow outdoors in early April and transplant in June for cropping in August-September.
Autumn varieties: Sow outdoors in April-May and transplant in late June.
Winter varieties: Sow outdoors in May and transplant in July.

	JAN	FEB	MAR	APR	MAY	JUN	JUL	AUG	SEP	OCT	NOV	DEC
Recommended Sowing Time				PP	PP	P	P					
Actual Sowing Dates												
Expected Picking Time	WINTER vars.					SUMMER vars.			AUTUMN vars.			
Actual Picking Dates												

CELERY

SEED FACTS

Celery seed is treated to prevent leaf disease, so do not use leftover seed in the kitchen.	
Expected germination time:	16–25 days
Amount to buy for 100 plants:	$\frac{1}{32}$ oz
Expected yield from a 30 ft row:	40 lb
Life expectancy of stored seed:	4 years
Approximate time between sowing and picking:	28 weeks

SOIL FACTS

All varieties require a sunny site and well-prepared soil. For Self-blanching types dig thoroughly in April, incorporating liberal quantities of manure or compost. For Trench varieties dig a 'celery trench' in April and allow it to settle until planting time. Rake in a general fertilizer before planting.

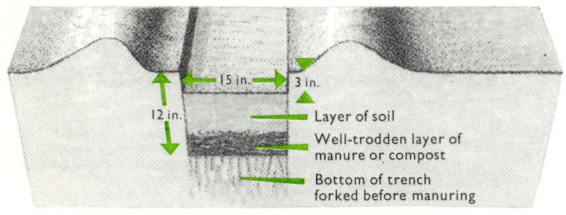

Diagram labels: 15 in.; 3 in.; 12 in.; Layer of soil; Well-trodden layer of manure or compost; Bottom of trench forked before manuring

SOWING AND PLANTING

Sow seed under glass and harden off the seedlings before planting outdoors. Self-blanching varieties are planted 9 in. apart in a square block (not in single rows) so that the plants will shade each other. Trench varieties are set out at 12 in. intervals in the trench. Fill the trench with water after planting.

LOOKING AFTER THE CROP

* Put down Slug Pellets. Celery is a thirsty and hungry crop – water copiously in dry weather and liquid feed with Bio Plant Food or Fillip during the summer months.
* If brown blisters (Celery Fly) appear, pick off the affected leaves and spray the plants with malathion.
* Blanch the Trench varieties once they are 12 in. high. Remove any side shoots, wrap the stems with newspaper, tie loosely and replace soil taken from the trench. In late August mound moist soil against the stems and in mid September complete earthing up to give a steep-sided mound with only the foliage tops showing.

HARVESTING

Lift the Self-blanching varieties as required. The Trench varieties are ready for harvest 8 weeks after the start of blanching. Begin at one end of the earthed-up row. There is no need to wait for a sharp frost; despite popular tradition frost does not improve crispness.

VARIETIES

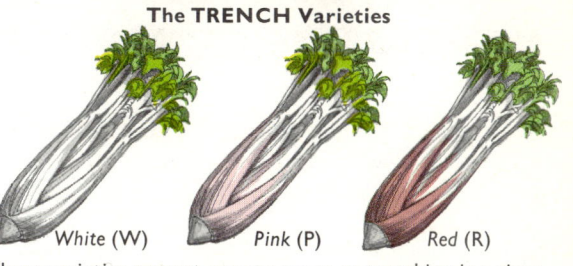

The TRENCH Varieties

White (W)   Pink (P)   Red (R)

These varieties are not easy to grow, as trenching is a time-consuming job. Choose from this group if you are an exhibitor or if you have rich, deep soil. Otherwise grow Self-blanching celery.
The white varieties have the best flavour but are the least hardy. Grow a pink or red celery if you want a late crop.

GIANT WHITE (W)
PRIZETAKER (W) Best exhibition celery
DWARF WHITE (W)
WHITE ICE (W)
HOPKIN'S FENLANDER (W)
GIANT PINK (P)
GIANT RED (R)
STANDARD BEARER (R)

The SELF-BLANCHING Varieties

Yellow (Y)   Green (G)

These varieties have taken the hard work out of celery growing. They require neither trenching nor blanching, and they mature before the end of summer. They are milder in flavour and less stringy than the Trench varieties. Their main drawback is the lack of winter hardiness.

LATHOM SELF BLANCHING (Y)
GOLDEN SELF BLANCHING (Y)
AMERICAN GREEN (G)
TENDERCRISP (G)
GREENSNAP (G)
GREENFAYRE (G)
UTAH (G)

Variety Grown	Flavour	Yield
Reminders for Next Year		

CALENDAR

Buy celery seedlings for planting in late May-early June or raise your own by sowing seed under heated glass in March or early April.
Self-blanching varieties will be ready for harvest between August and October. The Trench varieties are grown for winter use from October onwards.

	JAN	FEB	MAR	APR	MAY	JUN	JUL	AUG	SEP	OCT	NOV	DEC
Recommended Sowing Time			▨	▮	P	P						
Actual Sowing Dates												
Expected Picking Time	▮							▨	▨	▮	▮	
Actual Picking Dates												

page 15

GREENHOUSE CUCUMBER

SEED FACTS

Select the plumpest seeds for sowing	
Expected germination time:	3–5 days
Expected yield per plant:	5 lb
Life expectancy of stored seed:	6 years
Approximate time between sowing and picking:	10–12 weeks

SOIL FACTS

Virtually nobody devotes a whole greenhouse to cucumbers; they must fit in with other plants, especially tomatoes. A special soil mixture is required – 2 parts loam, 1 part compost and a cupful of sterilized Bone Meal per 2 gallons of mixture is ideal. Or use J.I. Compost No. 3. Set out the soil mixture in heaps along the border or on the staging at least 7 days before planting.

2 gallons of soil mixture
48 in.

Alternatively, grow plants singly in 10 in. pots filled with the soil mixture, or in pairs in a growing bag.

SOWING AND PLANTING

Sow seed ½ in. deep in 3 in. peat pots filled with moist soilless compost. Keep warm until germination and then maintain a minimum temperature of 60°F (70°F for All-Female varieties). Plant out seedlings into the soil mixture when they have reached the 4 leaf stage. Water well in.

LOOKING AFTER THE CROP

* Train the stem up a vertical wire or cane. Pinch out the top when the roof is reached. The side shoots are trained along horizontal wires placed about 1 ft from the glass.
* Female flowers have a miniature cucumber behind them. Male flowers have just a thin stalk. The tip of each side shoot is pinched out at 2 leaves beyond a female flower. All male flowers must be removed – fertilized fruit is bitter.
* Keep soil moist but not waterlogged. Never water right up to the stem. Keep the air as moist and well-ventilated as the other plants in the house will allow.
* Feed every 2 weeks when fruit begins to swell. If Whitefly appear, spray with Crop Saver.

HARVESTING

A pointed cucumber is immature; the sides should be parallel. Cut when the fruits have reached a reasonable size – if cucumbers are allowed to mature and turn yellow then cropping will cease.

VARIETIES

Greenhouse varieties are known as Frame Cucumbers.

The ORDINARY Varieties (O)

Green   *White*

These are the cucumbers of the exhibitor. They are the traditional cucumbers of the summer salad – long, straight, smooth and dark green. Old favourites, such as Telegraph and Butcher's Disease Resisting, still remain popular despite the advent of the new hybrids. There is a 'white' variety (Sigmadew).

The ALL-FEMALE Varieties (F)

These new F_1 Hybrid varieties have several advantages. As they bear only female flowers the tiresome job of removing male flowers is unnecessary. They are also highly resistant to disease and they are extremely prolific. There are two drawbacks – the fruits tend to be shorter than the Ordinary varieties and a higher greenhouse temperature is required. Examples are Topsy, Femdam, Femina, Feminex, Fertila and Simex.

For Top Flavour
Choose SIGMADEW (O)
        TOPSY (F)

For Cool Houses
Choose ORDINARY Varieties

For Houses Containing Tomatoes
Choose CONQUEROR (O)

For Exhibiting
Choose TELEGRAPH IMPROVED (O)

For Northern Gardens
Choose BUTCHER'S DISEASE RESISTING (O)

For All-Round Performance
Choose TOPSY (F)
        TELEGRAPH IMPROVED (O)
        BUTCHER'S DISEASE RESISTING (O)

Variety Grown	Flavour	Yield
Reminders for Next Year		

CALENDAR

Sow seed from February onwards, the most suitable time depending upon the amount of heat you can provide. A minimum temperature of 65°–70°F will be required at the start of growth, followed by at least 60°F for Ordinary varieties and 70°F for All-Female varieties.

	JAN	FEB	MAR	APR	MAY	JUN	JUL	AUG	SEP	OCT	NOV	DEC
Recommended Sowing Time		▨	▨	■								
Actual Sowing Dates												
Expected Picking Time					▨	■	■	■	▨			
Actual Picking Dates												

OUTDOOR CUCUMBER

SEED FACTS

Soak seed overnight before sowing	
Expected germination time:	6–9 days
Expected yield per plant:	25 cucumbers
Life expectancy of stored seed:	6 years
Approximate time between sowing and picking:	10–14 weeks

SOIL FACTS

A sunny spot protected from strong winds is essential, because outdoor cucumbers are not hardy plants. The soil must be well drained and very rich in humus. Most households will need only a few plants, so prepare 'planting pockets'.

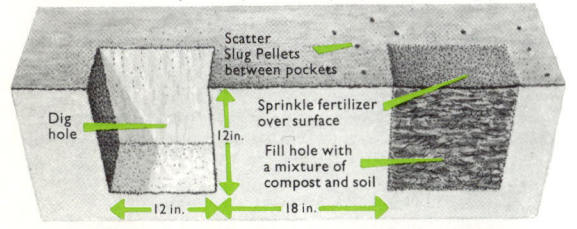

Diagram: Dig hole 12 in. deep, 12 in. × 18 in. Scatter Slug Pellets between pockets. Sprinkle fertilizer over surface. Fill hole with a mixture of compost and soil.

SOWING AND PLANTING

Sow 3 seeds 1 in. deep and a few inches apart at the centre of each pocket. After germination thin out to leave the strongest seedling. Alternatively, raise the seedlings under glass. Sow the seeds ½ in. deep in 3 in. peat pots filled with moist soilless compost. Harden off before planting in pockets outdoors. Disturb the roots as little as possible when planting out.

LOOKING AFTER THE CROP

* Pinch out the growing tip when the plants have developed 6–7 leaves. Lateral shoots will then develop, and these can be left on the ground or trained up stout netting. Any lateral not bearing fruit should be pinched out at the 7th leaf.
* Keep the soil moist. Water *around* the plants, not over them. Syringe lightly in dry weather.
* Once the fruit starts to swell protect from the soil with a tile or piece of wood. Start regular feeding with a liquid fertilizer.
* Never remove the male flowers; fertilization is essential for outdoor cucumbers.

HARVESTING

Don't try to grow record-breaking fruits. They should be cut before they reach maximum size, as this will encourage further fruiting.
The harvesting period is quite short, as the plants will be killed by the first frosts. Despite this, good soil and continuous picking will result in numerous fruits from each plant. Pick the Apple variety when it is the size of a duck's egg.

VARIETIES

Outdoor varieties are known as Ridge Cucumbers.

The ORDINARY Varieties (O)
These varieties are usually thick and medium sized, with a rough knobbly surface. They include the 'gherkins', such as Venlo Pickling.

The F_1 HYBRID Varieties (H)
These varieties have been bred to improve performance and hardiness (such as Burpee Hybrid) or to remove the acids which cause indigestibility (the Burpless varieties).

The JAPANESE Varieties (J)
The Japanese Climbing varieties include the longest and smoothest-skinned of all outdoor cucumbers.

The APPLE Variety (A)
This variety is extremely unusual – small, round and yellow. The flavour and juiciness, however, are outstanding.

For Top Flavour
Choose BATON VERT (H)
APPLE (A)

For Digestibility
Choose BURPLESS GREEN KING (H)
BURPLESS TASTY GREEN (H)

For Very Small Plots
Choose PATIO-PIK (H)

For Length of Fruit
Choose CHINESE LONG GREEN (J)
KING OF THE RIDGE (O)
KYOTO THREE FEET (J)

For Early Crops
Choose KAGA (J)
BATON VERT (H)
BURPLESS EARLY (H)

For All-Round Performance
Choose BEDFORDSHIRE RIDGE (O)
BURPEE HYBRID (H)

Variety Grown	Flavour	Yield

Reminders for Next Year

CALENDAR

Sow outdoors in late May. In the Midlands and northern areas cover the seeded area with cloches for a few weeks. Cropping should start in early August.

For an earlier crop sow seeds under glass in late April and plant out the seedlings in early June.

	JAN	FEB	MAR	APR	MAY	JUN	JUL	AUG	SEP	OCT	NOV	DEC
Recommended Sowing Time					P							
Actual Sowing Dates												
Expected Picking Time								■				
Actual Picking Dates												

KALE

SEED FACTS

Keep watch for new varieties of this 'Cinderella' vegetable	
Expected germination time:	7-12 days
Approximate number per oz:	7000
Expected yield per plant:	1½ lb
Life expectancy of stored seed:	4 years
Approximate time between sowing and picking (Early varieties):	30 weeks
Approximate time between sowing and picking (Late varieties):	36 weeks

SOIL FACTS

Kale is much more accommodating than the other brassicas, such as cabbage, cauliflower and brussels sprouts. It will grow successfully in nearly all soils.

Don't dig the land before planting out kale; merely remove any weeds and rake in a little fertilizer. Lime if the land is acid. The land must be firm – that is the only rule.

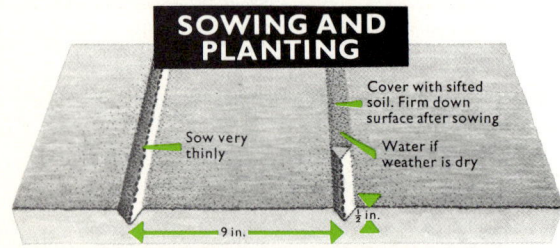

SOWING AND PLANTING

Sow very thinly. Cover with sifted soil. Firm down surface after sowing. Water if weather is dry. 9 in. apart, ½ in. deep.

When the seedlings are about 6 in. high they are ready to be transferred to the spot where they will grow to maturity. Choose a day after it has been raining and plant the seedlings *firmly*, leaving 2 ft between them.

LOOKING AFTER THE CROP

* Hoe regularly to prevent weeds and tread firmly around the plants to prevent them rocking in the wind.
* Kale is remarkably resistant to several brassica troubles, such as Cabbage Root Fly and Club Root. But Mealy Aphid and White Fly can be a nuisance, and so can Cabbage Caterpillars. Spray with Crop Saver at the first sign of attack.
* Rake up soil around the stems in autumn.

HARVESTING

There is more skill in harvesting kale than in growing it. Start at the crown of the plant, pulling off a few young leaves each time you pick. Discard all yellowing leaves.

This partial stripping of the crown will stimulate the development of succulent side shoots and these should be gathered *young*. If left to mature they will be bitter when cooked.

The flavour is improved once there has been a hard frost.

VARIETIES

Kale has nearly all the attributes of the ideal winter vegetable – extreme hardiness, tolerance of poor soil conditions and a prolonged cropping period. Its lack of general popularity arises from its poor flavour reputation. This is largely due to the incorrect practice of using large leaves or large shoots for cooking. Pick only small and tender "greens" for kitchen use.

The CURLY-LEAVED Varieties
These 'Scotch' kales dominate the seed catalogues and are much more popular than the other types. Each leaf has an extremely frilled and curled edge, giving a parsley-like appearance. Good varieties are Dwarf Green Curled, Tall Scotch Curled, Frosty, Verdura, Fribor and Toga.

The PLAIN-LEAVED Varieties
These tall kales tend to be coarser than the Curly-leaved varieties, but they are extremely hardy and prolific, and they are easier to keep pest-free. Hardy Sprouting and Cottager's Kale are examples.

The RAPE KALE Varieties
These kales provide young tender shoots between April and June, and are not grown like other varieties. They are sown where they will mature, as they detest transplanting. Examples are Asparagus Kale and Hungry Gap.

The LEAF & SPEAR Varieties
Pentland Brig is an F_1 hybrid of a tightly curled and the Thousand-Headed Kale. It produces young leafy shoots in spring and these are followed by broccoli-like spears.

For Very Small Plots
Choose DWARF GREEN CURLED
FROSTY

For Kale before Christmas
Choose VERDURA
DWARF GREEN CURLED
FRIBOR

For All-Round Performance
Choose PENTLAND BRIG
DWARF GREEN CURLED

Variety Grown	Flavour	Yield
Reminders for Next Year		

CALENDAR

Sow early-cropping varieties in April, leaving the later varieties until May. The correct time for transplanting is governed by the height of the seedlings rather than the date.

Rape Kale varieties are sown where they will grow to maturity. Make the seed drills 18 in. apart and thin to leave 2 ft between the plants.

	JAN	FEB	MAR	APR	MAY	JUN	JUL	AUG	SEP	OCT	NOV	DEC
Recommended Sowing Time						P	P					
Actual Sowing Dates												
Expected Picking Time												
Actual Picking Dates												

LEEK

SEED FACTS

Pelleted seed is available	
Expected germination time:	21 days
Amount to buy for a 30 ft row:	$\frac{1}{10}$ oz
Expected yield from a 30 ft row:	30 lb
Life expectancy of stored seed:	3 years
Approximate time between sowing and picking (Early varieties):	36 weeks
Approximate time between sowing and picking (Late varieties):	45 weeks

SOIL FACTS

Leeks do not require the same degree of high fertility as an onion crop, and they will grow in almost any soil provided it is neither highly compacted nor waterlogged. Ideally the land should have been manured for a previous crop; otherwise work in some peat or old compost when carrying out the winter digging. Rake in a general fertilizer shortly before planting.

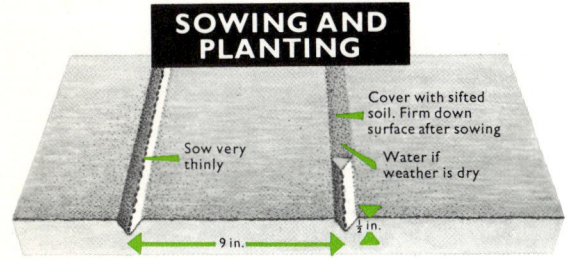

SOWING AND PLANTING

Sow very thinly. Cover with sifted soil. Firm down surface after sowing. Water if weather is dry. 9 in. ½ in.

The young leeks are ready for transplanting when they are about 8 in. high. Water the seedbed the day before lifting if the weather is dry. Plant in rows 12 in. apart, leaving 6 in. between the transplants. Note the special technique – make a 6 in. deep hole with a dibber, drop in the leek transplant and then gently fill the hole with water to settle the roots. Do not fill in the hole with soil.

LOOKING AFTER THE CROP

* Hoe carefully to keep down weeds, and make sure that the plants are not short of water during the summer months.
* To increase the length of white stem ('blanching') gently draw *dry* soil around the stems when the plants are well developed.
* A summer feed will increase the thickness of the stems.

HARVESTING

Begin lifting when the leeks are still quite small – in this way you will ensure a long harvesting period. Never try to wrench the plant out of the soil; lift it out gently with a fork. Leeks can remain in the soil during the winter months until they are required for use in the kitchen.

VARIETIES

The EARLY Varieties
SEPT OCT NOV

These varieties are popular with exhibitors as they can be sown under glass at the beginning of the year and they will reach their maximum size in time for the Autumn Show. Reliable examples are Marble Pillar, The Lyon, Prizetaker, Early Market, Malabar and Abel.

The MID SEASON Varieties
NOV DEC JAN

These varieties mature during the winter months and Musselburgh, the most popular of all home-grown leeks, belongs to this group. Other examples are Walton Mammoth and Hubertus.

The LATE Varieties
JAN FEB MAR

These varieties are the most useful of all for kitchen use, since they mature between January and early April when other vegetables are scarce. You can choose from Yates Empire, Winter Crop, Royal Favourite and Malines Winter.

For Top Flavour
Choose MARBLE PILLAR
MUSSELBURGH

For Winter Hardiness
Choose GIANT WINTER
MUSSELBURGH
NORTH POLE

For Exhibiting
Choose THE LYON
PRIZETAKER
GIANT EXHIBITION

For Long Stems
Choose MARBLE PILLAR
EVEREST
MONT BLANC

For All-Round Performance
Choose MUSSELBURGH
WINTER CROP
THE LYON

Variety Grown	Flavour	Yield
Reminders for Next Year		

CALENDAR

For exhibiting in the autumn sow under heated glass in late January and plant outdoors during April.

For ordinary kitchen use sow outdoors in early spring as soon as the soil is workable (early March-mid April). Transplant the seedlings in June.

	JAN	FEB	MAR	APR	MAY	JUN	JUL	AUG	SEP	OCT	NOV	DEC
Recommended Sowing Time				P		PPP						
Actual Sowing Dates												
Expected Picking Time												
Actual Picking Dates												

page 19

LETTUCE

SEED FACTS

Don't sow too many at one time – just a very small row every few weeks	
Expected germination time:	7–12 days
Amount to buy for a 30 ft row:	$\frac{1}{8}$ oz
Expected yield from a 30 ft row:	30 heads
Life expectancy of stored seed:	3 years
Approximate time between sowing and picking:	8–14 weeks

SOIL FACTS

Three basic needs have to be satisfied to obtain good lettuces. The soil must contain adequate organic matter, it must not be acid and it must be kept moist throughout the life of the crop. For summer lettuce dig the soil and incorporate compost in autumn or early winter. Rake in Bromophos if soil pests are a problem. At sowing time rake the surface to produce a fine tilth and apply a general fertilizer. Spring lettuces can be grown outdoors in mild areas without glass protection, but they will not succeed in poorly drained or cold exposed sites.

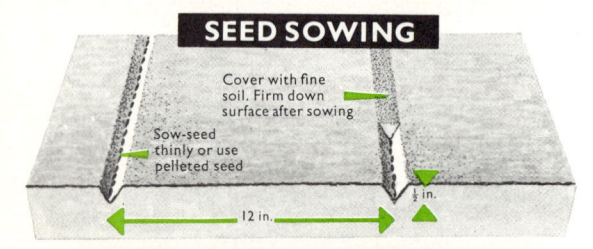

SEED SOWING

Cover with fine soil. Firm down surface after sowing

Sow seed thinly or use pelleted seed

12 in.

$\frac{1}{2}$ in.

LOOKING AFTER THE CROP

* Thin the seedlings as soon as the first true leaves appear. Avoid overcrowding at all costs. Continue thinning at intervals until the plants are 12 in. apart (9 in. apart for dwarf varieties).
* You can try transplanting thinnings in spring or you can plant shop-bought seedlings, but lettuces hate to be moved. Whenever you can, sow seed where the crop is to grow and mature.
* Put down Slug Pellets and protect seedlings from birds. Keep outdoor plants watered, but the soil under glass should be kept on the dry side. Ventilate glass-grown lettuce whenever possible.
* Greenfly can render the crop unusable; spray with Crop Saver. If Grey Mould strikes, then treat with Benlate.

HARVESTING

Lettuce is ready for lifting as soon as a firm heart has formed. If left for a few weeks the heart will begin to grow upwards, a sign that it is getting ready to bolt. You must then cut immediately for kitchen use or throw it away.
It is traditional to pick in the morning when the heads have dew on them. Pull up the whole plant and dispose of the root and lower leaves on to the compost heap.

VARIETIES

The CABBAGE Varieties

Butterhead (B) *Crisphead (C)*

The Butterheads are by far the most popular lettuce group. They are quick-maturing and the leaves are soft and smooth edged. Most of them are summer varieties; a few are hardy varieties which produce a spring crop and several are forcing varieties for growing under glass (for example Kloek, May King, Knap, Emerald, Kwiek and Premier).
The Crispheads produce large hearts of curled, crisp leaves. Examples are Webb's Wonderful and Avoncrisp.

The COS Varieties

Easy to recognize from their upright habit. Leaves are crisp and flavour is good.

The LOOSE-LEAF Varieties (L)

These varieties do not produce a heart. The leaves are curled and are picked like spinach – a few at a time without cutting the whole plant. Examples are Salad Bowl and Grand Rapids.

For Top Flavour
Choose BUTTERCRUNCH (B)
LITTLE GEM (COS)

For a Summer Crop
Choose WEBB'S WONDERFUL (C)
LOBJOIT'S GREEN (COS)
BUTTERCRUNCH (B)

For an Early Winter Crop
Choose KWIEK (B) Under cloches

For a Spring Crop
Choose VALDOR (B) Unprotected
WINTER DENSITY (COS) Unprotected
MAY KING (B) Under cloches

For All-Round Performance
Choose WEBB'S WONDERFUL (C)
BUTTERCRUNCH (B)
LITTLE GEM (COS)

Variety Grown	Flavour	Yield
Reminders for Next Year		

CALENDAR

For a Summer Crop: Sow outdoors in late March – late July for a June – October harvest.
For an Early Winter Crop: Sow a forcing variety in August. Cover with cloches in September for a November–December harvest.
For a Spring Crop: Sow a hardy variety outdoors in late August–September and pick in May. Or sow a forcing variety in early October, cover with cloches, and pick in April.

	JAN	FEB	MAR	APR	MAY	JUN	JUL	AUG	SEP	OCT	NOV	DEC
Recommended Sowing Time												
Actual Sowing Dates												
Expected Picking Time												
Actual Picking Dates												

MARROW

SEED FACTS

Soak seed overnight before sowing	
Expected germination time:	5–8 days
Expected yield from a 30 ft row:	40 lb
Life expectancy of stored seed:	6 years
Approximate time between sowing and picking:	10–14 weeks

SOIL FACTS

A sunny spot protected from strong winds is essential, because marrows are not hardy plants. The soil must be well drained and very rich in humus. Most households will need only a few plants, so prepare 'planting pockets'.

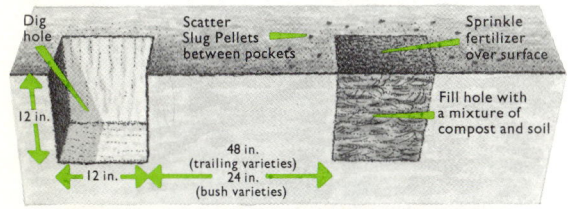

Diagram labels: Dig hole — 12 in. — Scatter Slug Pellets between pockets — Sprinkle fertilizer over surface — Fill hole with a mixture of compost and soil — 12 in. — 48 in. (trailing varieties) — 24 in. (bush varieties)

SOWING AND PLANTING

Sow 3 seeds 1 in. deep and a few inches apart at the centre of each pocket. After germination thin out to leave the strongest seedling.
Alternatively, raise the seedlings under glass. Sow the seeds ½ in. deep in 3 in. peat pots filled with moist soilless compost. Harden off before planting in pockets outdoors. Disturb the roots as little as possible when planting out.

LOOKING AFTER THE CROP

* Keep the soil moist. Water copiously *around* the plants, not over them. Syringe lightly in dry weather.
* Pinch out the tips of the main shoots of trailing varieties when they reach 2–3 ft long. Put down Slug Pellets at the first signs of leaf or fruit damage.
* Fertilize 2 or 3 female flowers (tiny marrow behind petals) with a male flower (thin stalk behind petals). Remove a mature male flower on a dry day, fold back petals and push gently into the female flower.
* Once the marrows start to swell feed every 14 days with Bio Plant Food or Fillip.

HARVESTING

Remove marrows for immediate use when they are still quite small — courgettes 4 in. long, marrows 8–10 in. long. Push your thumbnail into the surface near the stalk; if it goes in quite easily then the marrow is still at the right stage for summer picking. Continual cropping is essential to prolong fruiting. Take care when harvesting; cut marrows where they lie, *then* lift them away.
For pumpkins and marrows for winter storage, allow the fruits to mature on the plant and remove before frosts. Store in nets in a cool room indoors.

VARIETIES

There is no exact definition of 'marrow', 'squash' and 'pumpkin'. Within each of these groups there may be bush and trailing varieties. The trailing (or vining) marrows require plenty of room to spread, or they can be grown up fences and tripods if a small-fruited variety is chosen.

The MARROW Varieties

Includes the traditional vegetable marrow shape and also the globular and oval varieties which are grown for summer use.

Bush varieties:
GREEN BUSH (Best All-Rounder)
PROKOR (Early)
WHITE BUSH (Compact Early)
LITTLE GEM (Ball-shaped)

Trailing varieties:
LONG WHITE (Good winter storage)
LONG GREEN (Largest vegetable marrow)
VEGETABLE SPAGHETTI (Inside comes away just like spaghetti)

The COURGETTE Varieties

Varieties of ordinary marrows which have a compact habit and can produce many small fruits over a long period.
ZUCCHINI
GOLDEN ZUCCHINI (Yellow-skinned)

The SQUASH Varieties

This group includes the flat-shaped marrows which are so popular in the U.S. They are grown for summer use although some can be kept for winter use.
PATTY PAN
CUSTARD WHITE
CUSTARD YELLOW

The PUMPKIN Varieties

This group includes the traditional pumpkin shape and also the winter squashes. They are generally rather thick-skinned and usually very large. The Pumpkin varieties are grown to maturity on the plant and then cut for winter storage.
HUNDREDWEIGHT
GOLDEN DELICIOUS
MAMMOTH

Variety Grown	Flavour	Yield
Reminders for Next Year		

CALENDAR

Sow outdoors in late May. If possible cover the seeded area with cloches for a few weeks, especially if you live in a late-spring area. The first courgettes will be ready in July.
For an earlier crop sow seeds under glass in April — end of month if unheated. Plant out in early June.

	JAN	FEB	MAR	APR	MAY	JUN	JUL	AUG	SEP	OCT	NOV	DEC
Recommended Sowing Time				▨	■							
Actual Sowing Dates												
Expected Picking Time							▨	■	■	▨		
Actual Picking Dates												

ONION from Seed

SEED FACTS

Pelleted seed is available	
Expected germination time:	21 days
Amount to buy for a 30 ft row:	¼ oz
Expected yield from a 30 ft row:	22 lb
Life expectancy of stored seed:	1–2 years
Approximate time between sowing and picking (August-sown varieties):	46 weeks
Approximate time between sowing and picking (Spring-sown varieties):	22 weeks

SOIL FACTS

Exhibitors grow their show onions in a permanent bed. In the kitchen plot it is usually better to change the site annually. Choose an open, sunny spot if possible. Dig thoroughly in early winter, incorporating a liberal quantity of manure or compost. Before sowing or planting it is necessary to prepare the traditional 'onion bed'. Rake when the soil is reasonably dry, tread over the area to firm the surface and then rake again to produce a fine, even tilth.

SOWING AND PLANTING

Cover with sifted soil. Firm down surface after sowing. Water if weather is dry. Sow very thinly. 12 in. ½ in.

Thin the spring-sown crop in 2 stages, first to 1–2 in. and then to 6 in. apart. Lift the seedlings carefully—the soil should be moist and all thinnings removed to deter Onion Fly.
Seedlings raised under glass or from an outdoor August sowing should be transplanted 6 in. apart, leaving 12 in. between the rows. The roots must fall vertically in the planting hole, and the bulb base should be about ½ in. below the surface. Plant firmly.

LOOKING AFTER THE CROP

* Hoe carefully or weed by hand. Water in dry weather and liquid feed regularly.
* Break off any flower stems which appear. Stop watering once the onions have swollen and keep them exposed to the sun to ripen.

HARVESTING

When the crop is mature the foliage will topple over. Leave them for about 2–3 weeks and then carefully lift by hand or with a fork on a dry day. The crop is then dried and stored as described on page 23.

VARIETIES

The BULB Varieties

Flat (F)   *Globe (G)*

These varieties are grown for their large bulbs which can be stored throughout the winter months. Some have a flattened shape, others are globular. Skin colours vary from pale yellow to bright red and flavours range from mild to strong.

The SALAD Varieties (S)

Thinnings of the Bulb varieties can be used as "spring onions", but there are several varieties which are grown specifically for salad use. These Salad varieties, or scallions, are white skinned and mild flavoured. They can be sown from March to August to provide a long succession.

For Mild Flavour
Choose — RED GLOBE (G)
AILSA CRAIG (G)
YELLOW GLOBE (G)

For Salad Use
Choose — WHITE LISBON (S)
WHITE PORTUGAL (S)

For Exhibiting
Choose — SHOWMASTER (G)
AILSA CRAIG (G)

For Autumn Sowing
Choose — AUTUMN QUEEN (F)
EXPRESS YELLOW (G)
RELIANCE (F)
SOLIDITY (F)

For Long Storage
Choose — GIANT ZITTAU (F)
AUTUMN SPICE (G)
DURA (G)
RELIANCE (F)

For All-Round Performance
Choose — AILSA CRAIG (G)
BEDFORDSHIRE CHAMPION (G)
RELIANCE (F)

Variety Grown	Flavour	Yield

Reminders for Next Year

CALENDAR

In mild areas sow in August and transplant in mid March for bulb onions in July.
For an August-September crop sow as soon as the land is workable in the spring.
For exhibition-sized bulbs, sow in a heated greenhouse in January, harden off in March and plant outdoors in mid April.

	JAN	FEB	MAR	APR	MAY	JUN	JUL	AUG	SEP	OCT	NOV	DEC
Recommended Sowing Time			P	P								
Actual Sowing Dates												
Expected Picking Time												
Actual Picking Dates												

ONION from Sets

SET FACTS

'Heat treated' onion sets: the flower embryo has been killed to prevent bolting	
'Virus free' shallots: the stock is free from Virus Yellows	
Expected sprouting time:	11–14 days
Approximate number per lb (onion sets):	200
Approximate number per lb (shallots):	25
Expected yield from a 30 ft row (onion sets):	24 lb
Expected yield from a 30 ft row (shallots):	20 lb
Approximate time between planting and picking (onion sets):	20 weeks
Approximate time between planting and picking (shallots):	18 weeks

SOIL FACTS

All onion crops require good soil, but sets need neither the fine texture nor the high organic matter content demanded by seed-sown onions. Dig the ground in early winter and incorporate compost if available. Firm the surface before planting and rake in a general fertilizer such as Growmore or Crop Booster.

PLANTING

As soon as onion sets arrive unpack and spread out in a well-lit, cool place to prevent early sprouting. With onion sets and shallots trim off the dried stems which would attract birds.

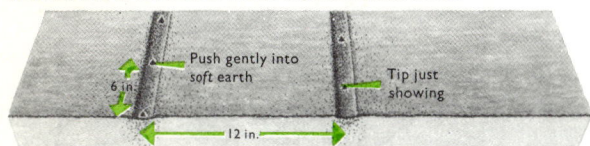

Push gently into soft earth — 6 in — Tip just showing — 12 in.

LOOKING AFTER THE CROP

✻ Firm the soil after planting. Protect from birds with black thread or netting if they are a nuisance in your area.
✻ Push back any sets which have been lifted by frost. Once the sets are established and shoots have appeared then treat the crop as for seed-sown onions (see page 22).

HARVESTING

Shallots: In June or July the leaves will turn yellow. Lift the bulb clusters and separate them, allowing each shallot to dry thoroughly. Remove the brittle stems and store in net bags in a cool, dry place. They will keep for about 8 months.
Onions: Lift the onions when mature (see page 22). They must now be dried, so spread them out in the sun if the weather is dry or in a greenhouse, cold frame or well-lit room if rain threatens. Use spotted, soft and thick-stemmed onions immediately. Store the rest in trays, net bags or as 'onion ropes'.

VARIETIES

ONION SETS

The onion sets you buy are immature bulbs which have been specially grown for planting. Shortly after being planted in the spring they start to grow again and eventually produce full-sized onions in September. There are several advantages in using sets rather than seed. They are quick-maturing, producing good-sized onions in cold areas where seed-sown crops might fail. They are not attacked by Onion Fly or Mildew, and they do not require rich soil for success. The main disadvantage until recently was their unfortunate habit of prematurely running to seed ('bolting'). But strains have been greatly improved, and bolting is no longer a serious problem.

Choose STUTTGARTER GIANT (Most popular)
STURON (High yielding)
RIJNSBURGER WIJBO (High yielding)
AILSA CRAIG (Old favourite)

SHALLOTS

The shallots you buy are already full-sized. When planted in early spring they quickly start to grow and eventually produce a cluster of 8–12 similarly-sized bulbs in July. These small bulbs are milder in flavour than onions and can be used for cooking, garnishing or pickling.

Choose DUTCH YELLOW
DUTCH RED

Variety Grown	Flavour	Yield

Reminders for Next Year

CALENDAR

Shallots should be planted very early in the season – mid February if possible, or during March if soil and weather conditions make it impossible.
Onion sets will give disappointing results if planted in cold soil. Plant them later than shallots – between mid March and mid April.

	JAN	FEB	MAR	APR	MAY	JUN	JUL	AUG	SEP	OCT	NOV	DEC
Recommended Sowing Time		P	P	P	P							
Actual Sowing Dates												
Expected Picking Time								■	■			
Actual Picking Dates												

page 23

PARSNIP

SEED FACTS

Seed is very light; sow on a still day	
Pelleted seed is available	
Expected germination time:	21–28 days
Amount to buy for a 30 ft row:	¼ oz
Expected yield from a 30 ft row:	30 lb
Life expectancy of stored seed:	1 year
Approximate time between sowing and picking:	33 weeks

SOIL FACTS

If you want to grow long and tapering parsnips then you will need a deep, friable soil which has been well manured for a previous crop. Almost any soil, however, will grow a good crop of one of the shorter varieties provided that you dig it deeply, refrain from adding any fresh manure or compost and then break down all the clods before seed sowing time. Add lime if necessary and finally rake in Crop Booster when preparing the seedbed.

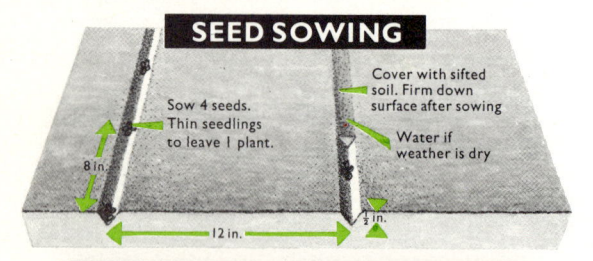

SEED SOWING

Sow 4 seeds. Thin seedlings to leave 1 plant.
Cover with sifted soil. Firm down surface after sowing
Water if weather is dry
8 in.
12 in.
½ in.

LOOKING AFTER THE CROP

* Parsnips seldom produce satisfactory roots after transplanting, so throw thinnings away.
* Hoe regularly to keep down weeds. The crop requires very little attention when it is growing and it is not usually attacked by pests or diseases. Carrot Fly can cause some damage and so can the leafmining Celery Fly. If blisters do appear on the leaves then squash them between the fingers and spray the plants with malathion.

HARVESTING

The roots are ready to lift when the foliage begins to die down in the autumn. The flavour is improved after the first frosts.
Lift the roots as required, leaving the remainder in the soil for later harvesting. It is a good idea to lift some in November and store as for carrots (see page 13). In this way you will have a supply of parsnips when the soil is frozen hard or covered with snow. Lift and store any roots which are still in the ground at the end of February.
Some of the parsnips may be forked. This is due to lumpy soil, stony soil or the presence of fresh organic matter.

VARIETIES

The popularity of parsnips continues to decline. They occupy the ground for a long time and when plain boiled provide a dish which is not to everyone's taste. But there are much more appetising ways of serving them, and the shorter varieties make success easier in a wide variety of soils.

The SHORT-ROOTED Varieties (S)

The shortest parsnip is the conical-shaped Avonresister. Choose it for poor soils, late planting or where Canker, the most serious of all parsnip troubles, is prevalent.

The INTERMEDIATE-ROOTED Varieties (I)

These medium-sized parsnips are generally longer than Avonresister and may be blunt-ended or tapered. A very useful group for general cultivation.

The LONG-ROOTED Varieties (L)

These are the straight and finely-tapered parsnips of the showbench. Unless you have a deep soil which is free from clay, you will have to sow in specially prepared 'soil pockets'.

For Top Flavour
Choose THE STUDENT (I)
OFFENHAM (I)

For Heavy or Shallow Soil
Choose AVONRESISTER (S)
OFFENHAM (I)

For Canker Resistance
Choose AVONRESISTER (S)
WHITE GEM (I)

For Exhibiting
Choose TENDER AND TRUE (L)
EXHIBITION (L)

For All-Round Performance
Choose AVONRESISTER (S)
OFFENHAM (I)
TENDER AND TRUE (L)

Variety Grown	Flavour	Yield
Reminders for Next Year		

CALENDAR

February is the traditional month for sowing parsnips, but the weather is usually far too unsettled to allow the production of the necessary fine seedbed. Wait until March when the soil is warmer, or even April if you are growing one of the shorter-rooted varieties.

	JAN	FEB	MAR	APR	MAY	JUN	JUL	AUG	SEP	OCT	NOV	DEC
Recommended Sowing Time		▨	■	▨								
Actual Sowing Dates												
Expected Picking Time	▨									▨	■	■
Actual Picking Dates												

PEA

SEED FACTS

Treat with a fungicidal seed dressing if sowing in cold soil	
Expected germination time:	7–10 days
Approximate number per pint:	1400
Amount to buy for a 30 ft row:	½ pint
Expected yield from a 30 ft row:	30 lb
Life expectancy of stored seed:	2 years
Approximate time between autumn sowing and picking:	32 weeks
Approximate time between spring sowing and picking:	12–16 weeks

SOIL FACTS

Peas are not an easy crop to grow, and under poor soil conditions the yield will be very disappointing. Choose an open spot which has not grown peas for at least the past 2 seasons. Dig the soil deeply in autumn or early winter, and incorporate compost into the top spit. Apply a light dressing of a general fertilizer shortly before sowing time.

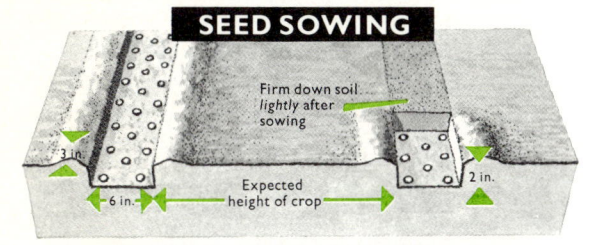

SEED SOWING

Firm down soil lightly after sowing
3 in.
6 in.
2 in.
Expected height of crop

LOOKING AFTER THE CROP

* Protect the rows from birds with either netting or black cotton before the seeds germinate.
* Hoe regularly to keep weeds under control. When the seedlings are 3 in. high insert short twiggy branches alongside the stems to provide support. Medium and tall-growing varieties will need extra support – place a strongly erected screen of plastic netting next to the row.
* Water during dry spells in summer. Apply a mulch of peat or grass clippings between the rows to conserve moisture.
* To avoid maggoty peas, spray with Kilsect 7–10 days after flowering.

HARVESTING

A pod is ready for picking when it is well filled but while there is still a little air space between the peas. Start picking at this stage, beginning at the bottom of the stem and working upwards. Use *two* hands, one to hold the stem and the other to pick off the pod.
Pick regularly; pods left to mature on the stem will seriously reduce the crop. If you harvest too many to cook immediately, then freeze or dry the remainder.
When all the pods have been picked use the stems for compost-making. Leave the roots in the soil.

VARIETIES

The ROUND Varieties (R)
Recognized by their smooth round seeds. Not many Round varieties appear in the catalogues, but they are the hardiest and fastest maturing of all peas.

The WRINKLED Varieties (W)
Recognized by their wrinkled seeds. These 'marrowfat' peas are sweeter, larger and heavier cropping than the Round varieties, and are therefore much more widely grown.
There are some interesting Continental types. Petit pois is the sweet french pea – look for Cobri or Gullivert.

The MANGETOUT Varieties (M)
There are several names for this group – Mangetout, Eat-all, Sugar Pea. Sow seed in March–June, pick the pods while the peas are still small and cook the pods whole – like french beans. Examples are Oregon Sugar Pod (4 ft), Carouby de Maussane (5 ft) and Dwarf de Grace (3 ft).

For Top Flavour
Choose HURST GREEN SHAFT (W) 2½ ft
HURST BEAGLE (W) 1½ ft
GULLIVERT (W) 3 ft

For a May/June Crop (Autumn Sowing)
Choose FELTHAM FIRST (R) 1½ ft
METEOR (R) 1½ ft

For a June/July Crop
Choose LITTLE MARVEL (W) 1½ ft
PILOT (R) 3 ft
ONWARD (W) 2½ ft
KELVEDON WONDER (W) 2 ft

For an August Crop
Choose SENATOR (W) 3 ft
ALDERMAN (W) 5 ft
ACHIEVEMENT (W) 4 ft

For a September Crop
Choose KELVEDON WONDER (W) 2 ft
PIONEER (W) 2 ft

For All-Round Performance
Choose KELVEDON WONDER (W) 2 ft
PILOT (R) 3 ft
ONWARD (W) 2½ ft
HURST GREEN SHAFT (W) 2½ ft

Variety Grown	Flavour	Yield
Reminders for Next Year		

CALENDAR

For a May/June Crop: Sow a suitable Round variety (see list) in October–November. Cover seedlings with cloches.
For a June/July Crop: Sow a Round or an early Wrinkled variety in March–April.
For an August Crop: Sow a maincrop Wrinkled variety in April–May.
For a September Crop: Sow a suitable Wrinkled variety (see list) in June–July.

	JAN	FEB	MAR	APR	MAY	JUN	JUL	AUG	SEP	OCT	NOV	DEC
Recommended Sowing Time			▨	▩	▨					▨	▨	
Actual Sowing Dates												
Expected Picking Time						▨	▩	▩	▨			
Actual Picking Dates												

POTATO

SEED FACTS

Do not plant diseased or rotten seed potatoes	
Amount to buy for 30 ft row:	5 lb
Expected yield from a 30 ft row:	45–65 lb
Approximate time between planting and harvesting (Early varieties):	13 weeks
Approximate time between planting and harvesting (Maincrop varieties):	22 weeks

SOIL FACTS

Potatoes can be grown in practically every soil type. It is the best crop to grow in grassland or wasteland which is to be turned into a vegetable plot. Choose a sunny spot if possible. Dig the soil in autumn and add peat or compost if the soil was not manured for the previous crop. Never add lime to the ground. Before planting rake in Bromophos if there is a wireworm problem, which is likely in newly-dug grassland. Break down any clods and sprinkle fertilizer over the surface.

PLANTING

As soon as you obtain your seed potatoes set them out in egg boxes (rose end uppermost) or in wooden trays containing a 1 in. layer of dry peat. Keep them in a light (not sunny) frost-free room so that there will be sturdy ½–1 in. shoots at planting time.

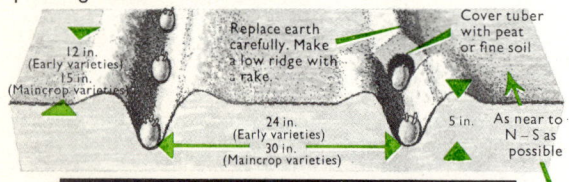

Diagram: Planting depth 12 in. (Early varieties), 15 in. (Maincrop varieties); spacing 24 in. (Early varieties), 30 in. (Maincrop varieties); cover tuber with peat or fine soil 5 in.; as near to N–S as possible; Replace earth carefully. Make a low ridge with a rake.

LOOKING AFTER THE CROP

* If there is still a danger of frost when the shoots have emerged draw a little soil over them for protection.
* When the haulm is about 9 in. high it is time for earthing-up. Break up the soil between the rows with a fork and remove weeds. Use a draw hoe to pile the loose soil against the haulm to produce a ridge 6 in. high.
* If the weather is dry, flood the trenches between the ridges. If the weather is wet in July, spray Maincrop varieties with Dithane to prevent Blight.

HARVESTING

With Earlies wait until the flowers or buds wither. Then carefully remove soil from a small part of the ridge and examine the tubers. They are ready for harvesting when they are the size of a hen's egg. Insert the fork into the ridge well away from the haulm. Lift the roots forward into the trench. With Maincrops for storage cut off the withered stems, remove them and wait 10 days. Then lift the roots and let the tubers dry for several hours. Then place them in a wooden box and keep them in the dark inside a frost-free shed.

VARIETIES

◀ rose end – most eyes occur in this area

Round (R)   Oval (O)   Kidney (K)

The EARLY Varieties
Earlies are grown to produce 'new' potatoes. These are immature tubers which can be easily scraped for cooking and possess a distinctive flavour when eaten hot or cold.

The MAINCROP Varieties
Maincrops can be lifted from August onwards but they are usually left to mature for storage in autumn. These varieties produce larger yields than Earlies, but are generally less popular with the home gardener. However, with the present price of potatoes the textbook recommendation that "they are not worth growing" no longer applies. As with Earlies, always buy 'certified' seed.

For Top Yields
Choose FOREMOST Early (O)
ARRAN PILOT Early (K)
PENTLAND CROWN Maincrop (O)
DESIREE Maincrop (K)

For Exhibiting
Choose HOME GUARD Early (R)
DR. MCINTOSH Maincrop (K)
CATRIONA Maincrop (K)

For Top Flavour (Boiled)
Choose EPICURE Early (R)
KING EDWARD Maincrop (K)

For Top Flavour (Chipped)
Choose KING EDWARD Maincrop (K)
MAJESTIC Maincrop (K)
KERRS PINK Maincrop (R)

For Top Flavour (Baked)
Choose GOLDEN WONDER Maincrop (K)
KING EDWARD Maincrop (K)
PENTLAND DELL Maincrop (O)

For All-Round Performance
Choose ARRAN PILOT Early (K)
DUKE OF YORK Early (K)
PENTLAND CROWN Maincrop (O)
DESIREE Maincrop (K)

Variety Grown	Flavour	Yield
Reminders for Next Year		

CALENDAR

Early varieties: Plant seed potatoes in early-mid April and harvest the 'new' potatoes in late June-July while the stems are still green.

Maincrop varieties: Plant in mid-late April and wait until the haulm has died down (September-early October) before lifting.

	JAN	FEB	MAR	APR	MAY	JUN	JUL	AUG	SEP	OCT	NOV	DEC
Recommended Sowing Time			▨	▨								
Actual Sowing Dates												
Expected Picking Time							▨	■	▨			
Actual Picking Dates												

RADISH

SEED FACTS

Pelleted seed is available	
Expected germination time:	4–7 days
Amount to buy for a 30 ft row:	$\frac{1}{6}$ oz
Expected yield from a 30 ft row (Summer varieties):	12 lb
Expected yield from a 30 ft row (Winter varieties):	30 lb
Life expectancy of stored seed:	4 years
Approximate time between sowing and picking (Summer varieties):	3–6 weeks
Approximate time between sowing and picking (Winter varieties):	10 weeks

SOIL FACTS

All gardening books will tell you that radishes require fertile, well-drained soil, rich in humus and free from stones. But radishes generally have to put up with what they are given. Despite this lowly status, they must be given some soil preparation to ensure the quick growth so necessary for tenderness and flavour. Dig in some peat or well-rotted compost. Apply a fertilizer before sowing and rake to a fine tilth.

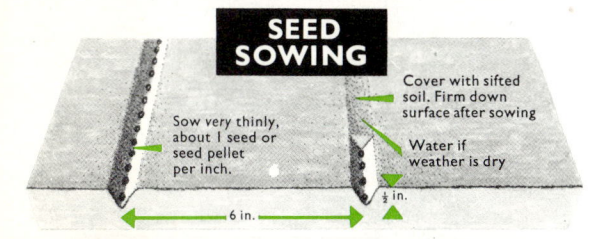

SEED SOWING

Sow very thinly, about 1 seed or seed pellet per inch.
Cover with sifted soil. Firm down surface after sowing.
Water if weather is dry.
6 in. / $\frac{1}{2}$ in.

LOOKING AFTER THE CROP

* With the Summer varieties little or no thinning should be necessary. If there is any overcrowding then thin immediately so that the plants are 1–2 in. apart. With the Winter varieties thin to leave the plants 8 in. apart.
* Protect the crop against birds. Spray with Derris or Crop Saver if Flea Beetle begin to perforate leaves.
* Hoe to keep down weeds. Water if the soil is dry; rapid growth must not be checked.

HARVESTING

Pull the Summer varieties when the globular ones are penny-sized and the intermediates are no longer than your thumb. They can, of course, grow much longer, but these overgrown specimens would be hot, woody and hollow.
The Winter varieties can be left in the soil and lifted as required during the winter. But it is better to lift them in November and store as for carrots (see page 13).

VARIETIES

The SUMMER Varieties

Round (R) Intermediate (I) Long (L)

This is by far the more popular group – the small radishes which garnish the salad plate. There are all-red varieties (Scarlet Globe, Inca, Red Forcing, Cherry Belle and Saxa), red-and-white varieties (French Breakfast, Sparkler and Half Long) and white ones (Icicle and Summer Cross).

For Mild Flavour
Choose ICICLE (L)
CHERRY BELLE (R)
SPARKLER (R)

For Sowing Under Cloches
Choose RED FORCING (R)
SAXA (R)

For Extended Harvesting
Choose INCA (R)
CHERRY BELLE (R)
SCARLET GLOBE (R)

For All-Round Performance
Choose CHERRY BELLE (R)
ICICLE (L)
FRENCH BREAKFAST (I)

The WINTER Varieties

This is a rarely grown group, and only a few varieties are available. The roots are large, weighing 1 lb or more, and these winter-maturing giant radishes are either finely sliced or grated for salads or cooked like turnips. They are generally stronger-flavoured than the small varieties.

Choose CHINA ROSE (I) 6 in. long
MINO EARLY (L) 12 in. long
ROUND BLACK SPANISH (R) 4 in. diameter
LONG BLACK SPANISH (L) 8 in. long

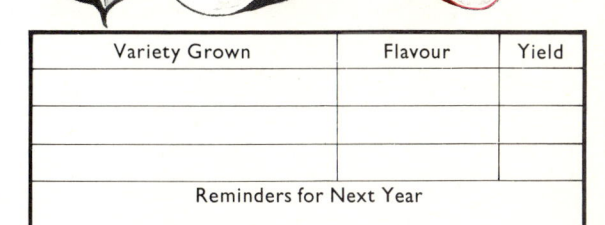

Variety Grown	Flavour	Yield

Reminders for Next Year

CALENDAR

Summer varieties: Sow under cloches in January-February or outdoors in March. For a prolonged supply sow every few weeks or try 'Mixed Radish' seed which contains varieties which mature at different times. Sowing after early June often fails.
Winter varieties: Sow in late July-mid August. Harvest roots from late October.

	JAN	FEB	MAR	APR	MAY	JUN	JUL	AUG	SEP	OCT	NOV	DEC
Recommended Sowing Time	▨	▨	■	■	■	■						
Actual Sowing Dates												
Expected Picking Time				■	■	■	▨	▨	▨	▨		
Actual Picking Dates												

SPINACH

SEED FACTS

Spinach seed is either round (Summer varieties) or prickly (Winter varieties)	
Spinach beet seed is similar to beetroot seed	
Expected germination time:	12–21 days
Amount to buy for a 30 ft row:	½ oz
Expected yield from a 30 ft row:	15–30 lb
Life expectancy of stored seed:	2 years
Approximate time between sowing and picking:	8–14 weeks

SOIL FACTS

Spinach is sometimes described as an easy vegetable to grow, but it can fail if the soil and position are poor. The ground must be rich and it should contain plenty of organic matter. Dig deeply in winter and lime if necessary. Apply Growmore or Crop Booster just before sowing time.

The ideal place for Summer spinach is between rows of tall-growing vegetables; the dappled shade will reduce the risk of bolting. Sow Winter spinach in a sunny spot which is protected from the wind.

SEED SOWING

Sow very thinly
Water before sowing
Firm down surface after sowing.
12 in.
1 in.

LOOKING AFTER THE CROP

* As soon as the seedlings are large enough to handle thin them to 3 in. apart. A few weeks later remove alternate plants for kitchen use. Leave remainder to mature.
* Hoe to keep down weeds. Water copiously during dry spells in summer. Spray with Crop Saver if greenfly become a problem.
* Winter spinach will need some sort of protection after the end of October unless you are lucky enough to live in a frost-free area. Use cloches or straw to cover the plants.

HARVESTING

Start picking as soon as the plants have reached a reasonable size. Always take the outer leaves, which should still be at the young and tender stage.

The secret is to pick continually so that fresh growth is encouraged. With Summer varieties you can take up to half the leaves on the plant without causing any damage; with Winter varieties pick much more sparingly.

Take care when harvesting. Cut off the leaves with fingernails or scissors – don't wrench them away which could damage the stems or roots.

VARIETIES

The SUMMER Varieties

These varieties have round seeds, and they grow quickly under good conditions to provide an early summer crop. Their main drawback is a dislike of hot and dry weather, when they rapidly run to seed.

LONG-STANDING ROUND (Good flavour)
BLOOMSDALE
KING OF DENMARK (Old favourite)
CLEANLEAF
MONARCH LONG-STANDING
DOMINANT
NOORMAN

The WINTER Varieties

These varieties have prickly seeds (exception – the round seeded Sigmaleaf) and they provide a useful harvest of winter greens. The modern varieties, such as Greenmarket and Virkade, have large leaves.

LONG-STANDING PRICKLY
BROAD LEAVED PRICKLY
SIGMALEAF (Long picking period)
VIRKADE
GREENMARKET

The NEW ZEALAND Variety

This is not a true spinach. It is a dwarf rambling plant with thick, fleshy leaves which are used as a spinach substitute. It is mild-flavoured and will not run to seed in hot, dry weather. Sow in late May and leave 3 ft between the plants.

The SPINACH BEET Variety

This type of beetroot (also known as Perpetual Spinach) is grown for its leaves. It is preferable to spinach in several ways, especially if your soil is poor or sandy. It will not bolt in summer nor freeze in winter and its flavour is usually more acceptable to children than true spinach. A single sowing should last a whole year.

Variety Grown	Flavour	Yield
Leaf Beet Perpetual	univus	
Reminders for Next Year		

CALENDAR

Summer spinach: Sow every few weeks from March to mid July for picking between June and September.

Winter spinach: Sow in August and again in September for picking between October and April.

Spinach beet: Sow in April and start picking in summer. The plants should continue cropping until early spring.

	JAN	FEB	MAR	APR	MAY	JUN	JUL	AUG	SEP	OCT	NOV	DEC
Recommended Sowing Time			▨	■	■	■	▨	■	■			
Actual Sowing Dates												
Expected Picking Time					▨	▨	▨			▨		
Actual Picking Dates												

SWEET CORN

SEED FACTS

Seed is large and easy to sow	
Expected germination time:	10–12 days
Amount to buy for a 30 ft row:	½ oz
Expected yield from a 30 ft row:	35 cobs
Life expectancy of stored seed:	2 years
Approximate time between sowing and picking:	15 weeks

SOIL FACTS

The situation is more important than the soil type. Choose a spot which is sheltered from the wind. Deep digging is useful, but do not incorporate fresh manure. You can dig in peat or old compost at this stage, but ideally the crop should rely on manure from a previous crop. Rake in Growmore or Crop Booster before sowing or planting.

SOWING AND PLANTING

Sweet corn must be sown or planted in rectangular blocks, not in single isolated rows. This will ensure effective wind pollination of the flowers.

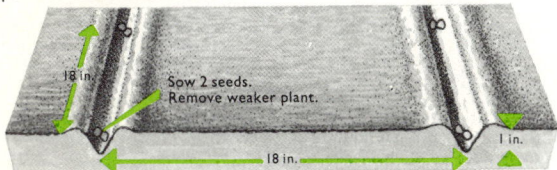

18 in. — Sow 2 seeds. Remove weaker plant. — 18 in. — 1 in.

Outdoor sowing is reliable in southern counties. In other areas sow outdoors under cloches or in 3 in. peat pots under glass, planting out when the danger of frost has passed. Leave 18 in. between the transplants and set the seedlings with their bottom leaves just above soil level.

LOOKING AFTER THE CROP

* Keep down weeds but do not hoe close to the plants or the shallow rooting system may be damaged.
* Roots will appear at the base of the stem; cover these with soil or a mulching of old compost. The side shoots ('tillers') which may develop should not be removed.
* Keep the plants well watered in dry weather. Liquid feed when the cobs begin to swell. Stake if plants are tall.

HARVESTING

Each plant will produce 1 or 2 cobs. Test for ripeness when silks have turned chocolate brown. Pull back part of the sheath and squeeze a couple of grains between thumbnail and fingernail. If a watery liquid squirts out then the cob is unripe. If the liquid is creamy then the cob is just right for picking. If the liquid is thick and doughy you have waited too long. Carefully snap the ear from the stem. Cook *immediately* for top flavour.

VARIETIES

Cob, Sheath, Grain, Tassel ('Silks')

The OLDER Varieties
These 'open-pollinating' varieties produce heavy crops, but they are not as reliable in our climate as the modern Hybrid varieties which have been specially bred for our type of conditions. The only popular example is Golden Bantam.

The F_1 HYBRID Varieties
These varieties have made it possible to grow sweet corn in nearly all parts of Britain.
The early-maturing types include:

JOHN INNES	(6 in. cobs)
FIRST OF ALL	(6 in. cobs)
POLAR VEE	(6 in. cobs)
EARLIKING	(7 in. cobs)
EARLY XTRA SWEET	(8 in. cobs)

Do not grow this variety near any other type of sweet corn — cross pollination spoils the flavour.

Later maturing types, which are generally taller than the early varieties, include:

KELVEDON GLORY	(8 in. cobs)
NORTH STAR	(8 in. cobs)

For Top Flavour
Choose: EARLY XTRA SWEET / HONEY DEW / KELVEDON GLORY

For Northern Areas
Choose: NORTH STAR / POLAR VEE

For Short, Compact Plants
Choose: FIRST OF ALL / JOHN INNES

For All-Round Performance
Choose: KELVEDON GLORY (for S. areas) / NORTH STAR (for N. areas)

Variety Grown	Flavour	Yield

Reminders for Next Year

CALENDAR

Southern counties: Sow outdoors in mid May; the cobs should mature during late August–September. For an earlier crop (late July onwards) sow under glass as described below.
Other counties: Sow under heated glass in mid April – early May and plant out in early June. Or sow outdoors under cloches in mid-May.

	JAN	FEB	MAR	APR	MAY	JUN	JUL	AUG	SEP	OCT	NOV	DEC
Recommended Sowing Time					▨ P							
Actual Sowing Dates												
Expected Picking Time								▨ ■ ▨				
Actual Picking Dates												

GREENHOUSE TOMATO

SEED FACTS

F₁ hybrid seed is available (see page 4)	
Expected germination time:	8–11 days
Expected yield per plant:	8 lb
Life expectancy of stored seed:	3 years
Approximate time between sowing and picking:	18 weeks

SOIL FACTS

Tomatoes can be grown in border soil—raised beds give better results than those at ground level. Prepare the soil in winter—dig in peat and a small amount of compost or manure. Rake in Crop Booster or Growmore shortly before planting. Unfortunately border soil soon becomes infested with soil pests and root diseases, so either the soil must be sterilized or changed after a couple of seasons. Alternatively you can grow the plants in 9 in. pots of soilless potting compost, in ready-prepared growing bags or by the ring culture method.

SOWING AND PLANTING

Sow the seeds in Bio Seed and Cutting Compost and keep at a minimum temperature of 60°–65°F. When the seedlings have formed a pair of true leaves prick them out into 3 in. pots filled with potting compost. At this stage they need plenty of light and a minimum temperature of 55°F. Plant out into the final quarters when the seedlings are about 8 in. high.

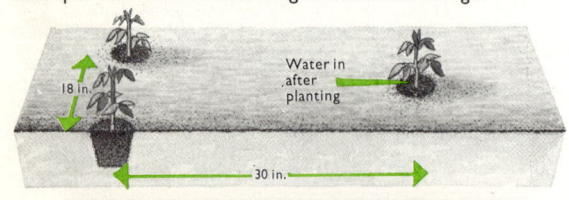

18 in. — 30 in. — Water in after planting

LOOKING AFTER THE CROP

* Tie the main stem loosely to a cane or wind it clockwise up a well-supported vertical string. Pinch out the growing tip when the roof is reached.
* Side shoots will appear where the leaf stalk joins the stem. Cut or pinch them out when they are about 1 in. long. Yellowing leaves below a ripening truss should be removed, but never overdo this 'deleafing' operation.
* Water regularly to keep the soil moist. Irregular watering will cause Blossom End Rot and Fruit Splitting. Feed with Bio Tomato Food every time you water. If using growing bags or pots you *must* water frequently.
* Spray plants occasionally to help fruit set. Artificial pollination is not required, but tapping the supports to aid pollen disposal is recommended.
* If Aphid or White Fly appear spray with Crop Saver.
* Shade the glass with Coolglass in summer and open ventilators when the temperature exceeds 70°F.

HARVESTING

Follow the rules set out for outdoor tomatoes (see page 31).

VARIETIES

The ORDINARY Varieties
This group of red salad tomatoes contains several old favourites which are grown for reliability (Moneymaker), flavour (Ailsa Craig) or earliness (Harbinger). Alicante is now very popular.

The F₁ HYBRID Varieties
This group bears fruit which is similar in appearance to the Ordinary varieties, but these modern crosses have two important advantages. They are generally heavier yielding and they have a high degree of disease resistance. Examples are Eurocross, Supercross, Ware Cross, Cura and Red Ensign.

The ONE POUND Varieties
These are the giants, reaching 1–1½ lb if the plants are stopped at the 3rd or 4th truss. Their meatiness makes them ideal for sandwiches. Choose either Big Boy or Spring Giant.

The NOVELTY Varieties
Several yellow varieties are available – Golden Queen, Golden Boy, Golden Sunrise etc. Tangella is orange, Tigerella is striped. They are not popular, yet their flavour is excellent.

For Top Flavour
Choose AILSA CRAIG
        HERALD
        PAGHAM CROSS

For Disease Resistance
Choose SUPERCROSS
        PAGHAM CROSS

For All-Round Performance
Choose ALICANTE
        AILSA CRAIG
        SUPERCROSS

Variety Grown	Flavour	Yield
Reminders for Next Year		

CALENDAR

In heated greenhouses, kept at a minimum night temperature of 50°–55°F, tomatoes are planted out in early March following a December sowing.

Most gardeners, however, grow tomatoes in an unheated ('cold') house. Sow seed in mid March and plant out in late April–early May to begin picking in July.

	JAN	FEB	MAR	APR	MAY	JUN	JUL	AUG	SEP	OCT	NOV	DEC
Recommended Sowing Time		▨	▨	P								
Actual Sowing Dates												
Expected Picking Time							▮	▮	▮	▮		
Actual Picking Dates												

OUTDOOR TOMATO

SEED FACTS

F_1 hybrid seed is available (see page 4)	
Expected germination time:	8–11 days
Expected yield per plant:	4 lb
Life expectancy of stored seed:	3 years
Approximate time between sowing and picking:	22 weeks

SOIL FACTS

Outdoor tomatoes are a tender crop, so choose a warm spot in front of a south-facing wall if you can. During the winter dig thoroughly and incorporate compost plus peat. Shortly before planting rake in a general fertilizer.

If you are growing only a few plants, or if you have no land available, then outdoor tomatoes can be grown in 9 in. pots filled with Bio Potting Compost or in ready-filled growing bags. Remember that this will call for much more frequent watering and regular feeding will be essential.

SOWING AND PLANTING

Raise seedlings as described on page 30. Alternatively, buy tomato seedlings for planting out. They should be dark green, sturdy and about 8 in. tall. Water the pots the day before transplanting and remove the soil ball gently. The top of the soil ball should be set just below the soil surface.

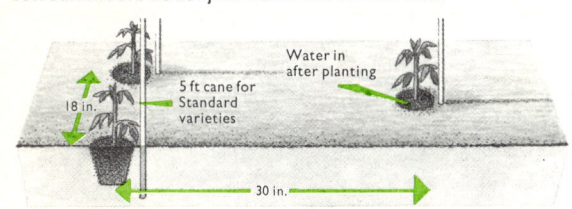

18 in. — 5 ft cane for Standard varieties — Water in after planting — 30 in.

LOOKING AFTER THE CROP

* If a Standard variety is grown loosely tie the stem to the cane. Make the ties at 12 in. intervals as the plant grows.
* Side shoots will appear where the leaf stalk joins the stem. Cut or pinch them out when they are about 1 in. long. Yellowing leaves below a ripening truss should be removed, but never overdo this 'deleafing' operation.
* When small tomatoes appear on the 4th truss remove the tip at 2 leaves above this truss.
* Aim to keep the soil moist. Alternating dryness with flooding will lead to Blossom End Rot and Fruit Splitting. Feed regularly with Bio Tomato Food.
* Syringe occasionally. Add Crop Saver if pests appear.

HARVESTING

Pick the fruit when they are ripe and fully coloured. Snap the stalk off the stem so that the calyx remains on the tomato. Although under glass you can continue to let fruit ripen on the plants when frosts threaten, the remaining green fruit outdoors should be gathered and ripened on a windowsill.

VARIETIES

The STANDARD Varieties (S)

These varieties are grown as single stems ('cordons') and they have to be trimmed and supported. The stem is stopped after the 4th truss has set so as to hasten ripening before the autumn frosts. There are many red varieties to choose from, including Gardener's Delight, Outdoor Girl, Moneymaker, Market King, Alicante, Ailsa Craig, Gemini, Ronaclave, Saint Pierre and Champion. There are yellow varieties (Yellow Perfection and Golden Sunrise) and the orange Tangella.

The BUSH Varieties (B)

These varieties make tomato growing extremely easy. They are either bushes 1–2½ ft high or creeping plants less than 9 in. tall. They do not require supporting or pruning, and are excellent for cloche culture. Their drawback is that the fruits are sometimes hidden, which makes harvesting more difficult than with Standard varieties. Straw or plastic must be laid round the plants as many fruits are at ground level. The Amateur is the most popular variety, but Sleaford Abundance and French Cross are also excellent varieties. Tiny Tim and Small Fry produce marble-sized tomatoes.

For Top Flavour
Choose GARDENER'S DELIGHT (S)
OUTDOOR GIRL (S)
PIXIE (B)
FRENCH CROSS (B)
SAINT PIERRE (S)

For Cool or Exposed Areas
Choose SUB ARCTIC PLENTY (B)
GEMINI (S)
RONACLAVE (S)

For All-Round Performance
Choose FRENCH CROSS (B)
OUTDOOR GIRL (S)
GARDENER'S DELIGHT (S)

Variety Grown	Flavour	Yield
Reminders for Next Year		

CALENDAR

Sow seed under glass in late March – early April and harden off during May. The seedlings are planted out at the end of May in southern counties, early June in more northerly areas. Plants to be grown under cloches are planted out in the middle of May.

	JAN	FEB	MAR	APR	MAY	JUN	JUL	AUG	SEP	OCT	NOV	DEC
Recommended Sowing Time					P	P						
Actual Sowing Dates												
Expected Picking Time												
Actual Picking Dates												

TURNIP and SWEDE

SEED FACTS

Don't sow too many early turnips at one time – just a very small row every few weeks	
Expected germination time:	6–10 days
Amount to buy for a 30 ft row:	¼ oz
Expected yield from 30 ft row (maincrop):	30 lb
Life expectancy of stored seed:	2 years
Approximate time between sowing and picking (turnips):	7–12 weeks
Approximate time between sowing and picking (swedes):	20–24 weeks

SOIL FACTS

Turnips require a rich well-manured soil, because flavour and tenderness depend upon quick growth. Before sowing early turnips in the spring, dig and incorporate compost or manure. Lime if necessary and let the ground settle before sowing. Turnips, like all brassicas, need firm soil.

Digging is not necessary before sowing maincrop turnips or swedes. Merely rake over the surface of land which has been cleared of a previous crop. Before planting any variety of turnip rake a general fertilizer into the soil surface.

SEED SOWING

Cover with soil. Firm down surface after sowing
Water if weather is dry
Sow seed thinly
15 in.
½ in.

LOOKING AFTER THE CROP

* Thin out the crop as soon as seedlings are large enough to handle. Do this in stages, until early turnips are 6 in. apart, maincrop turnips and swedes 12 in. apart. Do not thin turnips grown to provide "spring greens".
* Spray with Crop Saver at the first sign of Flea Beetle. Feed with Fillip, as turnips require boron.
* Keep the soil hoed and remember to water in dry weather. Rain following a dry spell causes roots to split.

HARVESTING

Pull early turnips when they are between golf ball and tennis ball size. Maincrop turnips can be left in the soil until required but in cold and wet areas it is preferable to lift them in early November. Remove the leaves and place the roots between layers of dry peat or sand in a stout box. Store in a shed and the crop will keep until March. Swedes can be left in the soil and dug up as required.

Turnip tops grown as "spring greens" should be cut when about 5 in. high.

VARIETIES

The EARLY TURNIP Varieties

Flat (F)   Cylindrical (C)   Globe (G)

These varieties are quick-maturing and should be pulled when the roots are still young and tender. They cannot be stored and should be used within a few days of harvest.

The MAINCROP TURNIP Varieties

Globe (G)

These varieties mature in mid October and they can be lifted and stored for use throughout the winter and spring. Turnip tops are the most nutritious of all "greens", and this group includes suitable varieties for this purpose.

The SWEDE Varieties

The swede is hardier and sweeter than the turnip. It will stand in the soil over winter and so lifting and storage are not necessary. Choose the old favourite Purple-Top or Chignecto (resistant to Club Root).

Choose	**For Top Flavour** GOLDEN BALL (Maincrop – G) SNOWBALL (Early – G)
Choose	**For Early Crops** PURPLE MILAN (Early – F) SPRINTER (Early – F) JERSEY NAVET (Early – C)
Choose	**For Winter Storage** PURPLE-TOP (Swede) GREEN-TOP STONE (Maincrop – G) GOLDEN BALL (Maincrop – G)
Choose	**For "Spring Greens"** GREEN-TOP WHITE (Maincrop – G) MARBLE-TOP GREEN (Maincrop – G)
Choose	**For All-Round Performance** TOKYO CROSS (Early – G) GOLDEN BALL (Maincrop – G) PURPLE-TOP (Swede)

Variety Grown	Flavour	Yield

Reminders for Next Year

CALENDAR

Early turnips: Sow in succession in April–July for a July–October crop.
Maincrop turnips: Sow in late July–mid August for cropping and storage from mid October.
Swedes: Sow in May–June for an October–March crop.
Turnip tops: Sow in late August–September for "greens" in March–April.

	JAN	FEB	MAR	APR	MAY	JUN	JUL	AUG	SEP	OCT	NOV	DEC
Recommended Sowing Time												
Actual Sowing Dates												
Expected Picking Time												
Actual Picking Dates												

CHAPTER 3
SPRAYING & WATERING

A prolonged dry spell can result in a small crop or even no crop at all. Heavy rain after drought causes the splitting of tomatoes and roots. Effective watering is the answer, and it is an art you must learn. Spraying against pests is another vital technique – the man who claims that he never needs to spray is either lying, lucky or living on poor vegetables.

WATERING is usually dealt with very briefly in handbooks on vegetable growing. The reason is quite simple – until the series of droughts in the 1970s many gardeners were able to succeed without watering their kitchen garden at all, apart from a little water around the roots of transplants.

The recent dry summers have illustrated why the U.S. and continental textbooks dwell on watering techniques at such length. Without adequate irrigation many crops will give bitterly disappointing results in a dry climate.

The first step is to incorporate adequate organic matter into the soil; this increases the water-holding capacity. Next, the top 1 ft of soil should be thoroughly and evenly moist but not waterlogged at sowing or planting time. Finally, put down a mulch (see page 34) in late spring.

You will have done all you can to ensure a good moisture status for your soil. The rest is up to the weather. If there is a prolonged dry spell then watering will be necessary, especially for potatoes, tomatoes, cucumbers, marrows, beans, peas, celery, young brassicas and onions.

The rule is to water the soil gently and thoroughly every 7–10 days. The soil will require at least 2 gallons per square yard when *overall watering*. Another technique is *point watering*, which involves inserting an empty plant pot into the soil next to each plant or creating a depression in the soil around each stem. Water is then poured into the pot or depression rather than over the whole area.

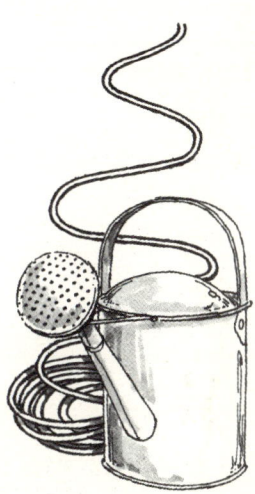

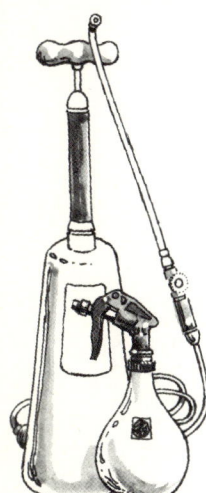

SPRAYING is an important part of the work which has to be done on the vegetable plot. Pests in the flower garden are unsightly; on food crops they are destroyers. Unfortunately, both pests and diseases will attack well-grown as well as sickly plants – strength and vigour do not produce immunity in plants any more than in humans.

There are a number of cultural ways apart from spraying in which you can keep down attacks. Carrot Fly and Onion Fly can often be avoided by sowing the seeds and handling the seedlings in the proper way. Always burn badly diseased plants and ventilate crops grown under glass. Feed and water as recommended because strong plants can withstand insect attack better than poorly-grown ones.

But pests will still come and you should be on your guard. Once a week look for the first signs of attack and be ready to take action immediately. Keep a sprayer and a multipurpose insecticide like Crop Saver handy. In this way Greenfly, Blackfly, Whitefly, Caterpillars, Flea Beetle, Pea Moth, Thrips, Weevils and so on can be dealt with promptly, and it is safe to pick the crop just a couple of days after spraying.

Systemic fungicides have added a new dimension to disease control. These sap-absorbed products, such as Benlate, are used to stop the spread of Grey Mould, Tomato Leaf Mould and Celery Leaf Spot. For Blight and Downy Mildew spray with Dithane.

Before spraying always read and follow the instructions on the bottle. After spraying wash out the sprayer and do not keep the liquid for use next week. Finally, note what you did in the table below for future reference.

DATE	CROP	PEST OR DISEASE	PESTICIDE USED	APPLICATION RATE	COMMENTS

CHAPTER 4
FEEDING & MANURING

Manure or fertilizer ... the age-old argument. Actually there is nothing to argue about; both are vital and neither can replace the other. The role of bulky organic matter is to make the **soil** good enough to support a vigorous and healthy crop. The role of fertilizers is to provide the **plants** with enough nutrients to ensure that they reach their full potential.

MANURING is the start of the gardening year. In autumn or early winter spread bulky organic matter over the soil surface at the rate of 1 barrowload per 10 sq. yards. The area chosen should be for crops other than roots or brassicas, unless the organic matter is well composted.

The two basic manures are garden waste compost and well-rotted animal manure. Other materials are hop manure and peat. The layer of organic matter is then dug into the soil, where it helps to improve the crumb structure and increase the water- and food-holding capacity.

It is vital that this manuring routine is carried out so that part of the plot is enriched each year until the whole area has been treated. Where land is short of organic matter and manuring is not carried out it is useful to line the drills with Bio Humus to provide a moisture-holding base for the seeds.

Do not add lime when manuring. You should lime *or* manure at digging time. In both cases fertilizer can be worked into the top few inches at the time the seed bed is prepared in the spring.

Mulching is an in-season method of manuring. A 1–2 in. layer of peat or well-rotted compost is spread between the plants after the end of April. Make sure the soil surface is moist and weed-free at the time of application. This mulch will conserve moisture and keep down weeds. It will also build up the organic content of the soil.

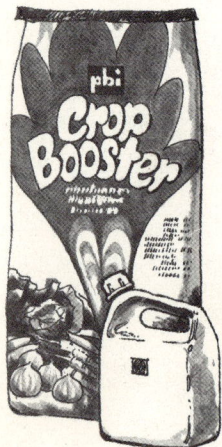

FEEDING is the application of nitrogen, phosphates, potash and/or trace elements to the soil or plants before or during the growing season. The purpose of fertilizers is to ensure rapid growth for enhanced flavour and high yields.

You will find a statement of the nutrient content on the package, and in this way you can compare one brand with another. Crop Booster is made specially for vegetables. Apart from nitrogen, phosphates and potash look for the extras, such as magnesium and trace elements. 'Organic base', however, can make virtually no contribution to the humus content of the soil.

The most important fertilizer treatment is the *base dressing*, which is applied just before or at sowing or planting time. Use a fertilizer which has slow-acting nutrients.

Crops which take some time to mature will need one or more *top dressings* during the growing season. These can either be in powder (keep off the foliage) or in liquid form. Bio Plant Food is diluted at the rate of 1 tablespoon in 1 gallon of water and applied to the soil through a watering can.

There is growing interest in the use of foliar fertilizers on the vegetable plot. These materials are sprayed on to foliage and are rapidly absorbed into the sap stream. This makes them independent of root activity, and so they work under a wide range of conditions. Fillip provides major nutrients and trace elements, and can be sprayed or watered on to small areas or applied through a Bio Hoser attached to a garden hose for large areas.

DATE	CROP	BASE OR TOP DRESSING	MANURE OR FERTILIZER USED	APPLICATION RATE	COMMENTS